THE NEW
ALCHEMY
Evolution of Our Future

THE NEW
ALCHEMY
Evolution of Our Future

BRAD CASSIDY

The New Alchemy: Evolution of Our Future, by Brad Cassidy

© 2025 Ronaye Matthew
Burnaby, BC

All rights reserved. No part of this book may be reproduced, stored in a retrieval system or transmitted, in any form or by any means, without the prior written consent of the publisher, except in the case of brief quotations, embodied in reviews and articles.

ISBN: 978-1-0696231-0-2 (paperback)
ISBN: 978-1-0696231-1-9 (ebook)

thenewalchemy.ca

I am

I am an expression of the resonances
of various forms of the great energy field

I am an anomaly,
and I am part of the greater unity

I am intended to exist,
and I am free to have my own intentions

I am unique and I am kin to all

I see my purpose as being all that I can be

To overcome the scars of the shame, hubris, hate
and isolation of my ego being

To bring my ego being into joyful, purposeful resonance
with the original silent self

To create myself whole,
that I might in some way by being so,
release energy back into the field to refine
and enhance the energy of my sphere

—Brad Cassidy, 1993

Contents

A Love Story ix
Ronaye Matthew

A Gift to Humanity xiii
Karl Buchner

A Scholar at Heart xv
Margaret Critchlow

Introduction 1
1. **The Invitation** 13
2. **Assumptions and Illusions** 35
3. **Being Human** 63
4. **Evolution of Western Culture** 97
5. **The New Alchemy** 129
6. **The Cosmology** 153
7. **Spirituality** 177
8. **Evolution of Our Future** 203

Glossary 215

A Love Story

by Ronaye Matthew

I met Brad in April 1994 at a personal development workshop called Come Alive at the Haven Institute on Gabriola Island, BC, Canada. The first moment I saw him, an unbidden realization came into my mind: *I have finally found you*. It was love at first sight. I was married to someone else at the time.

    I left my marriage, and Brad and I got together in September of that year. We spent 1995 doing intensive personal development work together at the Haven—essentially taking all the programs that the institute had to offer, supporting us to dive deep and bring consciousness to our lives and our relationship. It was an amazing start to an authentic, loving, and juicy partnership that lasted until Brad's passing in April 2023. I will miss him forever. And his passing has opened my heart to life in a way that I never could have imagined.

    This book is an act of love. It was inspired by a love for our species—a desire to support us to find a path of connection and to live to the fullness of our human potential. Although the book was not started in earnest until 2010, Brad had been preparing for it his entire life. He travelled extensively. He was a seeker, an explorer, delving into the human journey and attempting to find answers to the spiritual questions of life.

In many ways, this book is a mirror of our life together. I see myself reflected in his writing. I was working in the trenches in the human potential movement. Brad provided reflection and inspiration, supporting me to blossom in the fertile garden of our relationship.

I was devastated when Brad passed on April 10, 2023. My ground of being was shaken; my anchor to life was suddenly gone. I needed to find a path of reconnection if I was to continue my life's journey.

In May 2023 I began searching through Brad's computer files to try to locate his manuscript. I was aware that he had been very close to completing the book, but he had not shared it with anyone. His method of filing was very different from mine, so it required a creative leap to find what I believe were his final edits for each of the chapters.

I gathered all the chapters together and compiled them into an organized folder. Brad and I had been discussing the work for years, but this was the first time I had seen it in the written form. I shared the folder with a few close friends and family and asked if they thought it was worth the effort to publish. Five of the six readers thought it was brilliant. One reader was unable to see any possibility of a positive future for our species and stated there is nothing we can do—we are essentially flawed. Their response contrasted for me with something that Brad had said when we first got together: "I will continue to pump when the decks are awash; I will not go down without giving all that I have."

Four of us agreed to work together to prepare the book for publication. I have huge gratitude to Karl Buchner, Bonnie Corradetti, and Margaret Critchlow for their love, dedication, and willingness to volunteer their energy for this project. Karl took on the heavy lifting, doing the first structural edits and lassoing the book into a workable format. Margaret provided editorial review with her keen academic eye and attention to detail and clarity. Bonnie added her detailed review, ensuring readability and editing for continuity and syntax. I edited for succinctness and to make certain that Brad's voice was clearly illuminated.

I have immense appreciation for Jesse Finkelstein, Co-Founder and Co-CEO of Page Two publishing, who generously provided advice and support as we took the book to the final phase. Our copy editor Tilman Lewis, recommended by Jesse, was an absolute delight to work with, as was Michael Barker, our design consultant. I feel blessed to have been able to work with such caring and talented professionals.

The creation of this book was an alchemical process inspired by love. It welcomes us to open to a positive vision for our future.

A Gift to Humanity

by Karl Buchner

After expressing pleasantries at the opportunity of sharing over a lunch at our favourite bar, Brad would invariably open with "My past weeks have been focused on how the universe manifests its intent," or some similarly profound comment. I never ceased to marvel at his depth of insight into the human condition. Our merged minds would span hours on understanding human connectivity with all that exists, through to our contribution to the cosmic consciousness. I've never experienced such a profound bond with another.

His transformation from a rough and ready life in the forest industry to a visionary with phenomenal awareness of self is a journey few could even imagine, let alone achieve. As with everyone, our life is the sum of our decisions. In Brad's case, a midlife decision to pursue his destiny, versus his fate, as had been the case to that point, gave him the courage to overcome his subconscious ego fears and search for insight into his inner being, the true motivator of life's decisions. As with all, the universe presents opportunities. A chance encounter opened his awareness leading to his enrolment in a Come Alive program at the Haven, a frightening decision at the time. It was at this event that he met Ronaye, a fortuitous beginning along a lifestyle path toward self-actualization and becoming authentic.

In our sessions, he talked about his book, yet, despite offers, never shared his draft work. Upon reviewing his manuscript, I was shocked at his level of insight; it was a significant expansion on the topics of discussion over the years. I suspect his hesitation was a carryover of fears from his earlier years, the "I'm not enough" issue that haunts so many of us, myself included.

Humanity has lost a visionary and one of its finest gifts. I've lost a dear friend and partner in the universe's unfolding. May his spirit remain in the hearts and minds with those he touched and the readers of his insights for all time.

I miss him dearly.

A Scholar at Heart

by Margaret Critchlow

Brad Cassidy's intelligence, his curiosity, and his ability to educate himself supported him to write this bold, ambitious, and important book about humanity's future. This accomplishment is even more impressive in light of his limited access to scholarly resources. Brad did not have the privileges of an academic life or library. Professors like myself have access to the books, journals, and archives in scholarly libraries at their own and other institutions. We also have electronic access to a wide range of online libraries, research networks, and other collections. In contrast, Brad had none of the academic researcher's privilege, yet his brilliant and curious mind supported him to find all the information he needed in endless hours of research on his computer.

For Brad, like many scholars, research was in conversation with his writing, and both took years. Brad made excellent use of the sources he had available to support writing this book. It may be helpful to remember that this is not intended to be a comprehensive, scholarly account; rather, it presents a carefully reasoned argument. It makes a case for the capacity of the human spirit. For example, the condensed history of civilization Brad presents is in service to his larger goal, which is to show, despite the slowness with which human nature has changed, there is a vast evolutionary potential inherent in a humanity shaped by the loving nature of a universe that favours life.

When he graduated from high school, Brad's formal education came to an end, but in a sense, the end of his formal education was the beginning of his book. Brad travelled the world to get to know other ways of life, other people, and other cultures. He spent years in coastal BC doing hard physical work and connecting with "the bush" while pondering human nature. This book is the result of all that life experience combined with his extensive reading, internet-based research, and life-long study in personal development. Honed with his vision and wisdom, the book itself is alchemy. And it shows how alchemy can happen when the world needs it most: how the dross of contemporary humanity can become gold through the self-healing universe.

Brad was a natural anthropologist, fascinated by the diversity of cultural behaviour and beliefs. His lived experience, especially travelling in Asia, fed his curiosity. Hunter-gatherer societies particularly intrigued him, whether they were historical, prehistorical, or contemporary. Brad read and discussed all the anthropological literature on hunter-gatherers that he could get his hands on. At the time of his death, he was planning a trip to Namibia with his beloved wife and me, not to see the animals that attract so many tourists but to meet the people.

Soon after Brad passed, I had an uncanny experience, a strong sense that he and I were talking. In that conversation, it became clear to me how important it was to support finishing what he lightheartedly called his "magnum opus." With much appreciation for Ronaye's leadership and for being part of her editorial support team with Karl and Bonnie, I am delighted to see Brad's life's work completed with the publication of his book. He lives on in these pages.

Introduction

This book is about the path of human evolution: where our species has come from and where it may be going. Generally, the term *evolution* brings up thoughts of living organisms physically mutating to adapt to changing conditions or to exploit new environments, until finally, over millions of years, a new species arises. The focus of this inquiry, though, is the evolution of consciousness, culture, and self-perception in anatomically modern humans.

How did a few rather ordinary apes come down from the trees and eventually establish a high-tech, global civilization of eight billion members? Where are we today, what likely lies in our immediate future, and how might we best meet that future? What is essential to the nature of our species? What attributes have been gained and lost through the millennia? And finally, what would support our species to make a radical move forward and bring to fruition the promise and potential that lies latent within us?

This book has been inspired by the principles of alchemy, which Wikipedia defines as "an ancient branch of natural philosophy, a philosophical and protoscientific tradition that was historically practised in China, India, the Muslim world, and Europe." However, it is not about the old practice of alchemy.

Rather, the focus is on what can be gained from the old ways in order to forge new ones. Its principal assumptions are:

- there is an impending crisis,
- we humans have the creative potential to deal with the crisis, and
- positive evolution and change are possible.

In the relatively near future, we will face an unparalleled crisis resulting from a decrease in many of Earth's valuable assets and an increase in the corrosive factors: population, pollution, environmental destabilization, and so on. Without serious intervention to mitigate these trends, at some point the confluence of these elements will reach a critical mass and they will start to impact each other in unpredictable ways. The complexity of the factors involved, not the least of which is human behaviour, will result in chaos: massive disruption, destabilization, and potentially the collapse of global systems. It may be a crisis that decimates populations, reduces civilizations to ruins, and threatens humans with extinction. While the outcome is unknown, there is a strong prospect of a period of calamity, chaos, and suffering. It is no longer a question of whether a crisis will occur, but of when and how severe it will be. It is vitally important that we accept this situation for what it is and turn our attention to mitigating it.

To illustrate the problem, it is worth considering the concept of doom curves. In a graph of a doom curve, various factors converge, some increasing, others decreasing, until they meet and interact chaotically at a threshold point. The exact shape of the curve depends on the trends of the various factors, their relative importance, and their relationship to each other. But they trend inexorably to meet in an explosive crisis. On the decreasing side could be global weather stability, financial stability, security, access to energy, fecundity of the oceans, quality of soils, atmospheric quality, and so on. On the increasing side we would have population, terrorism, opportunism, pollution, fundamentalism, and other aspects. The point is not the details, it is the inevitability of a chaos event.

Many people with the clarity and courage to look at the depth of the crisis are inclined toward despair or suffer from fatigue and burnout due to deep underlying doubts about our collective ability to deal with its implications. One of the objectives of this book is to inspire faith in the collective human capacity. Acceptance of uncertainty plays a major role. The reality is: We cannot know our fate, but we cannot let uncertainty deter us. For those who wish to be part of the solution, we will be more able to sustain ourselves and serve our world if we accept uncertainty and hold a positive attitude about the potential outcomes.

There are many who believe sources outside of themselves will offer the necessary solutions to our problems, that science, politics, or divine intervention will save us from ourselves. I believe what is required is a mass transition of consciousness.

The need to take personal responsibility underscores the extraordinary fact that we humans, not just the forces of nature, have the potential to influence our evolutionary trajectory. This is an unprecedented situation for life on Earth. We can simply ignore this amazing chance and let things fall out as they may, or we can choose to consciously shift our way of being on an individual level to the extent that we shift the species' consciousness. We need enough committed individuals the world over to make this shift work.

If we are to be part of a change in consciousness, we need to put a priority on understanding, accepting, and developing ourselves on multiple levels. We must realize this is a critical priority. If we take on activism with our old patterns of adversarialism, fuelled by unresolved traumas and unconscious motivations, we will be perpetuating the mindset that got us into this global crisis in the first place. We will be acting out the same dominance dramas that have been with us since the Bronze Age.

I do not mean to suggest that we should step back from our work in the world until we have reached some grand state of enlightenment. What I am suggesting is that we put a focus on self-development and scrutinizing our actions and motivations as we work in the world. It is about raising our awareness, understanding what calls us to action, taking that action, and then assessing the outcome. This becomes a practice, a particular way of doing life, that can bring us to higher levels of functioning, creativity, and love.

When we seek a template for a new strategy, it is worth considering that the vast majority of human history has been an interaction between conservatism and radicalism. This interaction supports societies to maintain a dynamic balance that allows for slow, incremental progress. We continue to evolve, yet slowly. However, to achieve an epochal shift, incremental progress will not serve. What is required is a radical innovation, such as leaving the trees for the savannah or shifting from a hunter-gatherer society to an agricultural one. If we can develop a successful new strategy for our species, we will be propelled into the future at a higher operating level. If this is indeed an epochal cusp, we cannot assume that conservatism and stable incremental change will do us any good other than provide societal stability for a limited period of time. What is being called for is radical change.

THE NATURE OF THIS BOOK

When delving into realms of non-conventional thought, it is difficult to use conventional language to describe the concepts. When words have been used in a unique fashion, a brief definition is given in the text. There is also a glossary for easy reference, with links to some online sources.

Although this book includes an inquiry into our species' prehistoric past, and makes reference to general human nature and occasionally to various cultures, it is rooted in the Western world's history, culture, thought, science, and philosophy. This bias reflects the fact that the West's technical and economic success has invaded every corner of the globe. Many non-Western nations have adopted Western education, furthering this cultural invasion. Much of the human world is allowing itself to be seduced into the Western sphere and is, to varying degrees, adopting Western ways. In short, Western culture is, arguably, moving toward being the world culture.

In the coming times of change, much of the rest of the world will likely look to the West for methods, goals, and inspiration to cope with the epochal shift. If, and how, we change and adapt will set future global patterns. Therefore, the focus is on how Western history brought us to our present way of thinking/being and what aspects might be radically reassessed.

I make no attempt to present a scientific theory; this book is intended to be a modern natural philosophy in harmony with science. It goes beyond what science can presently prove or disprove and, therefore, can be neither endorsed nor dismissed by science alone. When this work goes beyond science, it does so not only because there are matters that science has not yet penetrated, but also because there are elements of human experience that are not suited to exploration by science. A popular quote often attributed to Einstein says: "Not everything that can be measured matters, and not everything that matters can be measured." Such intangibles as meaning, purpose, and the urge to understand and connect more deeply with the mysteries of life do not readily lend themselves to the scientific method. Science is powerful for investigation of the physical world, but when science is applied to the intangibles of life, it can result in distortions in perception and understanding.

Once we move past what science can readily explore and consider life's intangibles, we often encounter paradox. Western culture does not easily accept the uncertainty and ambiguity of unresolved paradox. Frequently, elaborate arguments are developed to resolve or dismiss paradox, leading to distortions of perception and understanding. A clear example of this is tragically expressed in our ongoing wars. While we say we long for peace, our propensity for violence and tribalism causes us to strive for peace by making war. When we ignore the fact that we contain within ourselves the paradox of both a peaceful and a murderous nature, we damn ourselves to cycles of war. Paradox is formed by the linear-thinking mind colliding with the multi-faceted matrix of experiential reality. Therefore, paradox is not an incomplete or flawed perception but, rather, a whole and natural phenomenon in itself.

One striking place where the issue of paradox shows up is in matters of spirituality. The previous example of the dual nature of peace/violence is similar to the concept of good/evil within us, a critical factor in how we understand and relate to ourselves and others. One of the great spiritual questions is whether humans are one unity or separate identities. How this question is answered has a huge impact on very practical matters in the world. Belief in the presence or absence of divine forces in the universe is a similar paradox, as are most of the great spiritual questions. The degree to which we can accept apparently mutually exclusive elements of a given paradox impacts the degree to which we can achieve sustainable outcomes that are in the best interests of the greatest number of people and the planet.

The term *spirituality*, as it is used in this book, refers to the nature of an individual's relationship to the intangibles of life and the cosmos. Thus, spirituality is a sister field to philosophy, with philosophy being more focused on the understanding of our relationship to the tangible and the concretely practical aspects of life, while spirituality holds within it all possible responses to an understanding of life's intangibles. Any belief system that represents the individual's point of view on these matters—whether it be religion, agnosticism, or atheism—falls under the category of spirituality. What is believed is immaterial; that there is a set of beliefs pertaining to the intangibles of life means there is a personal spirituality. While this definition may stretch how the word is commonly used, it serves to disentangle the modern concept of spirituality from a specific association with organized religion.

The spiritual perspective presented in this book assumes the first principle is cosmic love, comprising both the singularity that predated the Big Bang and the living, dynamic, creative forces of energy and consciousness that have given rise to reality. It is the ground of being—infused, embedded, and informing all that exists. All of what is within the cosmos, including us, is very much a part of it. The force of cosmic love could be thought of as divine, considering its universality, staggering immensity, and creativity. However, the term *divine* is likely to be confusing, as it is usually associated with an entity or entities (God; gods or goddesses) that created the universe and take a personal interest in sustaining that universe and caring for its creatures. While such an entity or entities could be possible, that is not how the term is used here. The concept of cosmic love rejects the idea of judgment, punishment, and redemption by the divine and assumes the cosmos is loving in a fundamental yet detached way.

WHY ALCHEMY?

Given the popular idea of alchemists as misguided proto-scientists, selfish seekers of magical gold, or outright con artists, why would alchemy be used as the primary theme, particularly when modern science has demonstrated that alchemy was at best a hit-and-miss approach to exploring the physical world? These popular conceptions of alchemy are simply not accurate. The true alchemists were dedicated spiritual seekers.

Alchemy is thought to have originated in three distinct regions, with an undetermined amount of cross-cultural influence or shared heritage between them. In each region, the various alchemical traditions had strong associations with local spiritual traditions: in China with Taoism, in India with the Vedic faiths, and in the Mediterranean Basin originally with Hermeticism and later with Christianity. It was in the cultural melting pot of ancient Alexandria that alchemy, as we know it in the West, was formed in tandem with its spiritual foundation, Hermeticism. Both were a syncretism of the wisdom of three great cultures: Egyptian, Greek, and Hebrew. They incorporated a range of principles and practices related to mythology, religion, spirituality, natural philosophies, and the technologies of the times. Alchemy was an intriguing combination of spiritual practices and physical experimentation. The physical aspect being an allegorical method for the description of, and a practical tool for attaining, the sought-after knowledge of the mysteries of nature and the divine. For this to make sense, we must keep in mind that through antiquity, until the Scientific Revolution took firm hold, most people did not separate matter and spirit as we do today. Rather, they saw the laws of nature as the laws of God or gods/goddesses. Clearly alchemy, in its higher form of practice, was seeking spiritual riches rather than material gains.

In the centuries between the advent of Hermeticism and the heyday of alchemy in the Renaissance, several transitions appear to have happened. Notably, although alchemy retained underpinnings of pagan Hermeticism, it became Christianized. It also became known, though poorly understood, by a broader segment of the population of the time. This made it possible for alchemists to be supported by the rich and royal, allowing them the security to expand their work. However, it also enabled opportunists to acquire superficial knowledge, giving rise to greedy gold seekers and con men. This is the reason why alchemical art and texts are so arcane—a deliberate attempt to protect the information from the ignorant and opportunistic. It was also, despite the intention to protect alchemical wisdom, the beginning of the misunderstanding of the nature of alchemy that persists to the present.

The higher process of alchemy was a spiritual pursuit in which the practitioner, through dedicated practice, sought direct personal insights into the mysteries of physical nature and the divine. This primary alchemical quest is the main reason why alchemy remains relevant in our time. Alchemy is first and foremost a call to spiritual and personal development—a message of critical importance to our species as we navigate the evolutionary leap before us. It carries a simple but profound message: through refining and developing our inner selves, we become increasingly empowered to create in the physical world. Furthermore, although alchemy proved to be inferior to science as a method for exploring the material world, much of lasting value was learned.

The following list outlines, in brief point form, some of the alchemical concepts that offer value to the modern seeker.

- **Teleology:** There is a purpose to the cosmos and all that is in it. Although it has been disdained by many in modern times, a reinterpretation of the underlying assumptions of the Big Bang, the fine-tuned universe, and the dynamic balance of the universe offers a strong validation for teleology.

- **Cosmic intelligence:** All things in the universe appear to be composed of ordered energy. Therefore, there is an ordering force that set up the laws of nature, which in turn gave rise to reality. This is the primordial cosmic intelligence that is embedded in all things.

- **As above, so below:** This is an ancient Sanskrit quote (circa 550 BCE) describing the idea that what happens in a higher realm or plane of existence also happens in a lower realm. It comes from an ancient piece of writing called the Emerald Tablet. The phrase is often associated with Hermeticism. This archaic maxim speaks to the self-similarity, unity, and harmony of the various levels of reality, from the subatomic through to the celestial.

- **As within, so without:** This phrase refers to the relationship between our inner and outer worlds. It is considered to be a universal truth or law that shows how our inner state of being affects our environment. What we see and experience outside of us is influenced by our inner thoughts, feelings, and beliefs. On the level of identity, this statement suggests that our inner being governs the type of subjective experience we create in our world. This is an important guide to how we might form the kind of world in which we want to live.

- **Duality and unity:** The old alchemy generally recognized that the union of opposites created a third entity. The Chinese Taijitu (yin/yang) symbol suggests that both opposites exist in one unity. Rather than seeing opposites as conflicting forces that should overcome each other, the Daoist principle of harmonious duality and the ancient alchemical tradition represent a worldview where opposites exist in harmony within a unified whole.

- **Transmutation:** A key alchemical principle, transmutation states that reality can be altered by a sufficiently advanced practitioner. While this concept fails on the physical plane (transmutation of metals), it remains valid for the transformations of emotions, attitudes, ideas, and societies.

- **Mystique:** The alchemists of old saw the world as alive, its elements having unique inner natures. All too common in current times is the concept that science has robbed the world of its wonder—a misinterpretation. A gift from alchemy is the call to see the world as purposeful, vibrant, and amazing.

The alchemists of old generally worked alone and for their own purposes. They made very little attempt to bring the spiritual wisdom they developed forward to the general population. Given the art's pagan roots and the attitude of the church of the time, their seclusion and secrecy are understandable. Nevertheless, there was more to their elitism. It was documented by some alchemical authors that the art was not for the common person, who was too ignorant and might misuse the insights or become frightened. Hence, alchemists stuck to themselves, and their art and literature were arcane. The attitude of that time needs to be consigned to the ash can of history. A revival of alchemical thought and attitude in our time could, and should, become a popular phenomenon where openness and honesty prevail.

There are several odd and unhelpful elements of the old alchemy that can be eliminated. But enough remains that is original, unique, and valuable to justify alchemy's rebirth in our time. The term *new alchemy* is intended to describe a modern, scientifically compatible model for a deeper and more heartfelt process of viewing and engaging with our reality. The intention of the new alchemy is to increase freedom, agency, and tolerance for all—a worldview to inspire a healthier, more sustainable world.

Chapter One

The Invitation

THE ANSWER LIES WITHIN

We humans have often looked for a source of help outside ourselves, for something that can lift us out of our feelings of overwhelm and helplessness, as though we can feel something out there much more powerful and better equipped to solve our problems than ourselves. Perhaps this is natural; feeling small in the face of the universe, we sense that there may be a consciousness present beyond our own. However, experience shows that desired outcomes based on hope alone seldom manifest.

Our species faces many serious threats to our survival at this point in our history: resource depletion, climate change, overpopulation, environmental degradation. These are problems we have brought upon ourselves. Many different external elements have been proposed as a catalyst for our redemption: the alignment of the heavenly bodies (Age of Aquarius), ancient prophecies (Mayan Calendar), and advents of the divine (Second Coming). But despite what has lined up, what has been foretold, or who is coming, we still seem to end up muddling through on our own. Redemption from our follies is not going to come by accident, oracle, or outside intervention—not even a divine one. We as a species need to wake up, mature, and take responsibility for our behaviours and the problems they create.

Whether you attribute human life to an accident of nature or to a divine intention does not change the fact that we have been gifted with amazing abilities and great potentials. We have used these gifts to survive in the face of physical adversity, predators, the ice ages, droughts, and a host of other challenges. As we moved past mere survival, we started to work on making life more secure and comfortable, eventually leading to the pursuits of beauty and learning. Within the last three thousand years, increased self-awareness has caused us to begin to study ourselves, the nature of reality, and the meaning of it all.

Yet there is a dark side within this evolutionary trajectory. It has been said that each person's greatest gift is also their fatal flaw—so too with our species. Along with the gifts of our complex minds and sensitive hearts, self-awareness has given rise to self-importance, egotism, and opportunism. The ability to imagine the future, to both plan for positive outcomes and foresee reasonable dangers, gave us greater control over our destiny, but it also gave us the capacity to imagine all sorts of unreasonable threats, impelling us to behaviours of greed, xenophobia, sexism, brutal repression, domination, and war. The human mind's ability to differentiate, sort, and label allowed us to lump things together or to separate them in ways that are either constructive or destructive. An example of a destructive application is the unfortunate behaviour of applying universal negative characteristics to all individuals of a group based on their race, sex, or religion, thereby condemning and separating them from others. The ability to intellectualize gives us the capacity to develop circuitous paths of so-called logic that lead to proofs, justifications, and rationalizations for negative behaviours and separation.

The mechanism that can counter these negative misappropriations is our human capacity for compassion. Although there has always been enough compassion, goodwill, and connection—coupled with our considerable ability to adapt and reproduce—to enable us to survive our foibles and even flourish, the ways of compassion have never been pre-eminent in the Western world. They have been ridiculed and shamed as a soft-heartedness that robs a person of their real power and ability to dominate. The cumulative effect of this attitude has gradually become monumental, species-wide, and global. These problems are so huge it is inconceivable that the thoughts, behaviours, and ways of being that created the issues can deconstruct them. Bringing the situation into a sane and sustainable state requires us to find a shared purpose to our collective humanity and to do the work that will support that transformation to happen.

The external elements are secondary to the primary task that requires attention, which is the internal. Even if we suddenly come up with an energy source that is clean and abundant, that will only delay the inevitable need to do the internal work. Our problems will not wait patiently for us: global climate change, overpopulation, and war will continue until a critical mass makes the necessary transition. The only major force for positive social change sufficient to the task lies with a raising of consciousness by a sufficient number of individuals to make a difference. All else is window dressing.

AN EPOCHAL SHIFT

An epochal shift is a quantum leap of consciousness that changes fundamental human behaviour, self-perception, and how life overall is perceived. Such a shift is not a simple change in material culture due to developing technology, nor is it an incremental shift in social consciousness that changes details of lifestyle. It is a whole different way of seeing ourselves, and our relationships to each other and to the environment, that creates a change in our identity and our perception of reality at its most primal level.

We stand on the cusp of an epochal shift the likes of which has not been seen since the Neolithic Revolution, when the economic change from hunter-gatherer to agriculture and the lifestyle change from nomadic to sedentary began. Social changes were coupled with these material changes, such as the stratification of society, the birth of national identity, militarism, and the codification of laws. We had a similar evolution before the Neolithic when our ancient ancestors descended from the trees, harnessed fire, and manufactured purpose-built tools. We collectively realized that we, unlike other animals, could deliberately manipulate aspects of our environment. Rather than happy accidents, these sorts of major events were probably responses to various kinds of stresses that had reached a point where failure to address them would have compromised our evolution. When the situation goes from stressful to unbearable or threatening, something will happen. The question is what.

The process of evolution described above is consistent with the theory of punctuated equilibrium, wherein the model is not one of slow, consistent, and incremental development over time, but more rugged progress through periods of relative stasis, minor change, and then profound radical transformation. In most cases, certainly within the Neolithic, radical change was spread over time and space. However, the impulse was so powerful that humans shifted in similar ways over a relatively short period of time spanning widely separated locations.

The two extremes of polarity anchor either end of a continuum of possibilities: a controlled process of radical change, innovation, and adaptation—or species extinction. The first possibility currently appears unlikely, given the general reluctance to deal with the known and evolving issues. The second scenario, species extinction, is somewhat mind numbing to consider, which is why so many people in our Western culture are in denial or despair. Unfortunately, denial and despair impede taking meaningful action, making the crunch, when it comes, all the more abrupt and severe. The more we delay taking action, the more we heighten the likelihood of collapse rather than a degree of controlled change.

Archaeological evidence of civilizations collapsing in the past indicates they were accompanied by massive reductions in population in specific global regions. In our situation, a full societal collapse would translate into mega-death, and the region would be the entire planet. The form, magnitude, and generalization of such an event could put our species' survival at risk.

Primary risks in our current time include resource depletion, war involving weapons of mass destruction, and monetary/political collapse. However, there are a lot of other factors that would likely come into play, making any one primary factor far more destructive than it might at first appear. One of these contributing factors is our huge population, particularly its concentration in urban areas dependent on layers of complex infrastructure. The failure of our infrastructure could result in famine, epidemics, and massive social disorder. Similarly, global climate destabilization could have significant effects on food production and sea levels. Resource depletion is likely to play a role in the crisis, particularly as shortages cause resource extractors to take greater and greater environmental risks to get what they want. If the political will is not there to contain this urge, we could be looking at multiple massive disasters that would further weaken our resilience. There is no need to wallow in the potential horrors that could befall us; it is sufficient to know that we will be facing them if we do not address the issues.

The idea of controlled, conscious change is certainly brighter, but even so, it stops short of being rosy. If we can move beyond denial, accept significant changes in our lives, and work together, we will be in a position to put the brakes on the descent of our civilization before it crashes completely. There are many variables involved in trying to imagine what this would look like. It depends greatly on the speed and severity of the challenges we face, how fast and how effectively we can respond, and how we behave under the stress. With so much uncertainty, it is pretty much impossible to predict when our world will decline into chaos. The timing of such an event, whether it is next week or two hundred years from now, is also pretty much a moot point. What matters is that the more effective our response to the situation is, the less devastating the chaos and upheaval will be. The less the devastation, the sooner we will be able to move toward establishing a sane, loving, and sustainable culture, a culture that would spread a sense of connection and shared destiny across the planet and finally unite our species.

There are many factors that will define the degree to which our response is effective. One of the primary ones is how quickly enough of us move out of denial and take the steps toward positive change. The sooner we respond, the longer and shallower the "crash curve" becomes—hence, a smoother transition. Fortunately, an untold number of groups, large and small, have begun the process of change, but a critical mass is needed. If we can achieve that, we will have the capacity to make the next great step of human evolution—an epochal shift in consciousness.

THE ROLE OF HUMAN EVOLUTION

The idea that a great step for our species can be stimulated by individual self-awareness brings up the question of how the evolutionary process relates to both individuals and our species. We need to not overlook the biological and structural aspects of the physical along with the associated evolving intellect, consciousness, and social and behavioural aspects.

In evolution, individuals are only important to the extent that they contribute to advancing the species. This is as true for the salmon that lays ten thousand eggs and dies, leaving its offspring to be reduced to a handful of returning adults, as it is for the doting parents of an only child. The life cycles, investment, and potentials may be very different, yet the principle is the same. Whether reproduction brings the return of one extraordinary salmon or the development of a single gifted child makes little impression on the species over time. What does matter is the consistent reproduction of many highly adaptive individuals. Simply put, in the big picture, it is not about me, it is about us. Although this is comprehensible, it is rather counterintuitive because our brain is organized in such a way as to make it appear that we are the centre of the universe. This is simply how we order reality. Our self-focus is important to both our individual selves and to the species, because it supports our survival; after all, without individuals there can be no species.

However, the production of unique individuals is itself a keystone to the evolutionary process. It is in the unique set of potentials and attributes of individuals that new and potentially adaptive characteristics are found. The reproductive process brings two unique sets of chromosomes together to form a third: a blending of the two original individuals to yield one-of-a-kind offspring to be tested for fitness in the environment. This process occasionally produces little glitches in the genetic code that create mutations and can cause changes in the offspring such that they carry characteristics previously unseen in the species. These changes are not always adaptive, but when they are, they can give a reproductive advantage to the individual, making it more likely for that trait to go forward in the gene pool. Cumulatively, it is these mutations that cause the species to evolve. Thus, the success of the individual serves the betterment of the species.

As far as we know, we are the only species that thinks about these things, a feature that puts us in a unique position to consider the future trajectory of our evolution. Prior to acquiring the ability to reason, the various impetuses that drove adaptive changes were on a level below that of our consciousness. This is no longer entirely the case; our ability to project into the future and to analyze and hypothesize potential outcomes began to be applied to philosophical matters in the 1st millennium BCE, the formative period for the world's religions, and that changed the game.

Fundamentally we are adapting ourselves over time to a changing environment, as all creatures are. However, there are two major differences at this time in our evolution. First is our level of consciousness and the capacity it gives us to change things. Second is the radically different environment that we humans have created—we are no longer entirely natural animals.

This change in adaptation is because much of our environment is created, maintained, and controlled by humans for our own purposes. Furthermore, a good percentage of this environment is made up of intellectual and social components. The manufacturing and maintenance of a controlled artificial environment is supported through relentless resource extraction, to the point of endangering our primary source. However, if we can manipulate our environment, we can also bring about changes to our relationship with it. We are in a position to make amends and improvements, which gives us an unprecedented power to chart our future course. We are the first creatures on Earth with the ability to use our consciousness to direct our evolution. The ability to consciously manipulate elements of our environment does not give us the power to override the natural order. Rather, it gives us the opportunity to consciously harmonize with the systems of nature.

In evolution, creatures that fail to adapt to the changing world die. If enough individuals die, the species slips under the reproductive threshold and goes extinct. Along the timeline of a species' evolution, some losses or failures to thrive are typically unavoidable. However, with human beings, this is no longer entirely so; our ability to control our environment and deploy our technologies has allowed us to correct for deformities and deficiencies in individuals, populations, and locations. Our capacities have removed us from the common lot of other animals; we are no longer operating under the same natural constraints that have previously shaped us and trimmed our populations.

When a species within a finite system becomes more numerous than the resources to support them, drastic reductions in population or extinction will occur. This can be seen in the process of fermentation: when the yeast consumes all the nutrients (sugars) in the vessel (its environment) and has filled it with its waste (alcohol), its population goes into sharp decline and then dies (in the fermentation vessel). We need to keep this principle in mind, for we, too, are living in a closed environment—the biosphere. Unlike the yeast, we are aware and must be very conscious of the fact that our huge and ever-growing population threatens us.

Being guided by the straightforward rules of the natural evolutionary process and applying reason and compassion to our policy-making can support us to develop adaptive strategies that may not guarantee our survival and success, but will make a positive outcome more likely. For instance, if we bear in mind that infinite population growth in a finite biosphere is dangerously maladaptive, then it would make sense to do everything we reasonably and compassionately can to ultimately reduce human population. If, on the other hand, we succumb to fear and turn to greed, opportunism, nationalism, and fundamentalism, we are sure to push the chance of a global civilization collapse past the point of no return. Our future, within the bounds of the natural order, is ours to decide.

A sizable part of the world is built, controlled, and maintained by us for the purpose of satisfying our needs. We have the chance to re-create the human world with focused functional processes that support us to reduce our demands for resources and bring us into a healthier balance with the greater environment. With collective wisdom and courage, we could be moving steadily toward a world that is peaceful, sustainable, and creative. Nature, through evolution, is indeed putting pressure on us to raise our consciousness and put ourselves in resonance with cosmic love.

UNIVERSAL NEEDS

Maslow's hierarchy of needs is an idea proposed by American psychologist Abraham Maslow in his 1943 paper "A Theory of Human Motivation" in the journal *Psychological Review*. This well-known classification system is intended to describe the universal needs of society as its base, then proceed to more acquired emotions. In Maslow's theory, physiological needs take precedence. Until such time as the physiological needs are adequately met, it is unlikely that a human being will spend much time or energy on anything other than self-preservation. However, once these physiological needs have been met, Maslow proposed that there are non-physical needs that impact human behaviour and motivation.

Despite the many differing ways these needs may be expressed in any particular individual or context, the adequate satisfaction of universal needs is critical to high functionality and happiness. In general, the people best able to make significant positive contributions to the external world are those who have sufficiently satisfied these needs. The capacity to contribute lifts the concept of universal needs out of the sphere of intellectual theory and places it in the realm of practical strategies for human progress.

The details of the theory are not important. Just how many specific needs there are and what we call them really depends on semantics and whether broad and general categories are preferred or many detailed ones. What is important is the idea that human beings have a group of primal needs common to all members, and that meeting those needs in a healthy and direct way is essential for individuals to reach their best potential.

One way to express these needs, listing a selection of primary satisfactions and compensations for each category, is shown in the table of Universal Human Needs (pages 24–25). This is a synthesis that comes from multiple resources and my experience working with people in personal development.

Why should meeting our natural universal needs be difficult and cause us to avoid direct satisfaction and instead seek the comfort of compensations? As social animals with a long period of dependency after birth, humans are influenced by our primary caregivers and, for the rest of our lives, remain susceptible in varying degrees to external influences. The avoidance of direct satisfaction happens during our socialization when we learn to repress unapproved emotions, block impulses, and deny aspects of our more primal (authentic) selves. These become the internal, self-imposed roadblocks that keep us from going directly to the satisfaction of our needs. There are also external, societally imposed roadblocks stemming from the need to conform and be successful in the outer world. As a result, direct satisfaction is often redirected toward something compensatory.

The point of discussing universal needs is to establish the idea that although we may need to look at giving up various presumed rights, long-held beliefs, behaviours, and opportunities, there are other sources of nourishment and fulfilment to replace those drives. Some of the things humans have avidly sought are little more than compensations for the lack of direct satisfaction of our universal needs. Perhaps some of the costs we imagine we will incur in the coming changes are actually golden opportunities to discover safe, sane, and mutually respectful ways of finding deeper satisfaction to our real needs.

Universal Human Needs

Safety	Appropriateness
Constituent Issues • Mental stability • Relational stability • Freedom from terror • Peace of mind *Primary Satisfactions* • Psychologically supportive environment • Sound relationships; Clear perceptions • Self-awareness; Knowledge • Friendship *Compensations* • Dependency; Isolation • Substances; Insanity • Delusions; Dissociation • Compulsions	*Constituent Issues* • Self-worth • Self-compassion • Love of others • Love of life/universe *Primary Satisfactions* • Positive mirroring • Accurate self-image • Spiritual connection • Felt sense of self *Compensations* • Hubris; Agency • Fanaticism; Martyrdom • Self-denial; Tyranny • Self-hate; Depression
Competency	**Love(d)**
Constituent Issues • Self-care • Autonomy • Contributing • Doing *and* being *Primary Satisfactions* • Achievement • Recognition • Nourishment (various) • Completion *Compensations* • Workaholism • Grandiosity • Dependency • Fraud	*Constituent Issues* • Love of self • Love of others • Being loved • Friendship *Primary Satisfactions* • Intimacy; Connection • Service; Appreciation • Receiving; Spirituality • Sharing; Altruistic acts *Compensations* • Domination; Transference • Withdrawal; Hatred • Pursuit of wealth • Sexual addiction

Creativity	Belonging
Constituent Issues • Self-expression • Service • Contribution • Learning	*Constituent Issues* • Relationships • Identity • Interdependence • Boundaries
Primary Satisfactions • Authentic expression; Gifting • Legacies • Education/teaching • Construction/creation	*Primary Satisfactions* • Connection; Social contract • Sharing; Receiving • Service; Humanism • Self-definition; Commitment/ acceptance
Compensations • Withholding • Devaluing • Shoddy proliferation • Plagiarism	*Compensations* • Patriotism; Enmeshment • Isolation; Tyranny • Power and prestige • Hyper-independence

Meta-aesthetic	Meaning
Constituent Issues • Harmony • Cooperation • Egalitarianism • Altruism	*Constituent Issues* • Faith • Purpose • Spirituality • Identity
Primary Satisfactions • Altruistic acts; Social service • Humanitarianism; Tolerance • Self-improvement • Environmental service	*Primary Satisfactions* • Spiritual connection; Faith experience • Contribution • Goals • Balanced cosmology
Compensations • Disdain • Destructiveness • Bigotry • Opportunism	*Compensations* • Nihilism • Denial • Fanaticism/fundamentalism • Delusions

CHANGE

We are on the cusp of a period of upheaval and chaos, the degree of which is indeterminable. Given the nature of the multiple stressors that will evoke a chaotic world state, maintaining the status quo would be highly maladaptive and likely catastrophic. Radical change will be required.

Population

The only way of reducing and stabilizing the human population without massive human suffering is to radically reduce the birth rate. Many people long to have children and grandchildren. There are cultures and religions that encourage their members to reproduce, and it is generally seen as a natural right. Both the desire and the notion of the rightness of reproduction has served our species throughout most of our existence. It is only in the very recent period of our evolutionary history that the situation has reversed, and we have not yet responded to this change.

We do not have to respond to the ancient imperative to reproduce; birth control is now well within our abilities. The question is whether we will have the vision, awareness, and compassion to put aside our desires and traditions in favour of the future of our species, our natural environment, and the other creatures we share that environment with. We can make demands on our governments to offer various forms of support, such as education, subsidies, or tax advantages, but attempts in the past to make contraception a law have resulted in negative social consequences and suffering. This is a personal decision that can only arise through increased consciousness.

Wealth

Global market data indicate that immense personal wealth exists in the world today, with the top 1 percent controlling nearly half, while much of the world's population struggles to make ends meet. This inequality has far-reaching implications, from the ability to access basic necessities to the ability to pursue educational and career opportunities. And it highlights the need for greater economic justice and a more equitable distribution of resources.

If we were to deconstruct military defences worldwide, how much wealth would be freed up? Thousands of billions of dollars are spent on defence every year, and massive resources are frozen in place by pre-existing military expenditures. There would also be savings through eliminating the hidden price of human and environmental destruction caused by military endeavours.

In addition to redistributing wealth, a reduction in global population would have a major impact on average wealth. If coupled with an increase in education and opportunity, there would be a notable increase in the creativity and productivity of the population overall, resulting in a stable sustainable population partaking in the world's wealth in an equitable manner and enjoying a reasonable standard of living.

Wealthy Western nations have laboured under the illusion that wealth equals success and happiness, and that more wealth translates into greater happiness. This is a cultural myth, and like all good myths, it contains some truth. However, for many it is not true. We need only to look at the incidence of depression, addiction, and isolation in Western societies as proof. It is relatively rare to meet a genuinely happy person living their life with purpose and receiving the joy and satisfaction that comes from the wealth model. If further evidence is necessary, it can be found by travelling to less wealthy regions and noting that the people generally show higher levels of good cheer, meaning, and social connection than in the West. This clearly reveals that beyond a threshold of basic necessities, there is no direct correlation between wealth and happiness.

So, why do we keep acting like there is a correlation? The lust for wealth is actually a compensatory addiction—a substitution for the very thing it is supposed to create. This mechanism is not limited to acquiring wealth as a substitute for happiness; it can also be seen as a substitute for power, love, or the need for prestige. These and many other examples illustrate the common habit of finding an alternative for one or more of the universal human needs that we believe are otherwise limited or unavailable. However, as finding an alternative to real needs does not speak directly to the actual need, it can never give more than a temporary feeling of fulfillment. This leads to the need to get more of the compensatory item, such as money, and very often these dynamics exhibit acquired resistance to the compensation, which means we continue to need more.

Up to a reasonable limit, wealth does serve our overall well-being. We can seek an adequate, average level of wealth for everyone, supporting those in need to gain the genuine benefits of wealth, such as improved health, security, and education. Many of us in the Western world need to recognize that acquisitiveness and materialism are not serving our real needs. Real happiness, satisfaction, purpose, and meaning arise when we meet our universal needs directly, and the degree of success depends on how directly and consistently we can do this within our given context.

Implementing radical strategies would be complex and challenging. It will have to come from an overall intention driven by an awakened population that calls into formation new social structures. It may not bring the collective standard of living up to what many in the West presently enjoy, yet the alternative is likely humanity's extinction.

Power and Prestige
Closely related to the lust for wealth is a longing for power and prestige based on a belief that our worth in the world is set by what we have done, what we possess, or how influential we are. Such beliefs are incompatible with wealth parity, real democracy, and egalitarianism. For those who believe that power and prestige are necessities, new social ideals could be seen as a serious threat that is worthy of active resistance.

The origins of the longing for power and prestige lie in the early adaptive strategies of our ancestors, when we competed for dominance to gain a mate, protect the group, and gain leadership to preserve the group or for some other purpose. On this level, an individual would primarily serve the group but, in the process, would receive some personal benefits such as identity, or a sense of belonging and contribution. These benefits are important non-material needs, which have an intrinsic value to members of our species that helps us to remain mentally healthy, connected, and motivated to serve. People who put themselves forward for little or no gain in wealth, prestige, or power get their nourishment from the satisfaction of inner needs. However, there are many who gauge every move in order to advance their own self-interests. Yet again, this is a situation where previously adaptive strategies have become dangerously maladaptive because humans and their context have changed so radically in the last ten thousand years.

Individualism and Independence
Many may fear that a truly egalitarian world would rob us of our individuality and independence—characteristics that are particularly prized in the West. In the case of individuality, we encounter a paradox. Our experience of physical autonomy and psycho-emotional separation feeds the belief that we are fully separate and individual. However, the fact remains that we

are similar and connected to every other human being on virtually every aspect including genetics, fundamental behaviours, and the collective unconscious (a term introduced by psychologist Carl Jung). This sets up the mentally challenging state of paradox where both contradictory states, autonomy and connection, are indeed true, and both need to be considered to fully recognize the situation.

Independence is simply a cultural myth. Our species evolved in interdependent groups, relying on each other every step of the way. Regardless of how we live, we remain in an interdependent state with other human beings.

As always, it seems there is another side to the coin. We have a need for a sense of autonomy, competence, and identity—part of the cluster of non-material needs that we all share. To define what is genuine need rather than a compensatory myth, we must be aware of the paradox of individuality and see that it plays a governing role in how we perceive and live our independence. If the world is to change toward greater equality and sustainability, we will not be losing our individuality and independence but re-evaluating them in light of the deeper needs they serve in our lives. These deeper non-material needs and our tendency to create compensations for their lack of fulfillment are important considerations.

THE REWARDS

Let us assume we make all the necessary sacrifices—we seek the methods and go through the process to become as strong, mature, and actuated as we can be. What then? Like many profound endeavours, the essence is quite simple: It changes us and we change the world. When we consciously push our own personal development forward, face our demons, accept our potentials, and deal with the great challenge of being a human being, the shifts that occur within us change how we relate to all aspects of life.

There are essentially four great relationships in life:

- relationship to self, which covers all internal relational aspects including self-awareness, self-image, self-knowledge, and self-compassion,
- relationship to others, which ranges from how we treat our significant other to how we interact with our species as a whole,
- relationship to nature, and
- relationship to the divine, which is our understanding of the mysteries of life and includes religion, philosophy, spirituality, cosmology, and more.

As we progress with our individual evolution, we begin to see ourselves differently, often developing far more appreciation for ourselves, and this appreciation displaces the feelings of inadequacy or the absurd compensation of vanity. The sense of empowerment supports purpose, focus, and faith in our ability to contribute to our own lives and the world around us. Interestingly, when we drop our dysfunctional defences and coping strategies in favour of simpler, healthier ones, we often free up a great deal of energy, both psychic and physical.

When our relationship to ourselves improves, our relationship to others and society also improves, because of the sense of belonging that a self-actuated individual can feel. It may seem paradoxical, but an increase in self-reference and autonomy can free an individual to become open to an enhanced connection with those around them, because a greater sense of self counteracts the fear of being subsumed by something larger than ourselves. We can become free to join the group without losing ourselves and to embrace life fully without being overwhelmed. The desire to belong is innate, and although how that need is fulfilled may vary between individuals, its satisfaction strengthens and nourishes each one of us. It is a remedy for the common feelings of alienation that plague and depress many in our society. Being able to belong and yet retain our autonomy frees us from dependence on external sources of influence from peers, heroes, and patriarchal leaders, while at the same time enhancing our capacity to become sensitive to external needs and information. In addition, an increased sense of belonging awakens our expanded worldview and deepens our connection to the natural world, inspiring us to cherish and protect it. Being more of who we are brings us into greater resonance with the divine that called us into being, resulting in a greater sense of meaning, clearer purpose, an increased sense of the appropriateness of life, and deep nourishment.

A benefit to our relationship with society is the call to serve as one becomes self-actualized. This is an innate calling, a legacy of our long history as social animals, and satisfying the calling strengthens us. Serving has been shown to have both health and social benefits along with lending purpose to our lives and simply bringing us joy. Society is a mass mirror of its individuals—the healthier the individuals within a society, the healthier the society. In practical terms, healthy, self-actuated people need less in the way of frivolous goods, services, and distractions, freeing resources to be applied to more constructive social uses. This is further supported by a reduction in mental and physical health care costs, reduced losses of productivity, and a lessening of numerous social ills and their resulting costs.

With healthier individuals contributing to a healthy society, and a healthy society supporting healthier individuals, we would have an up-spiralling societal well-being and functionality. Consciously pursued, we could make this the most accelerated period of human development in history—a happening that would go a long way to preparing us for the coming upheavals and changes to our world. This enhanced state of being supports an environment for a positive future outcome that is uplifting. It constitutes the most pragmatic adaptive strategy for our species. Enhancing and supporting the personal development of the individual is the invitation of our era, and it is a calling to each of us.

Chapter Two

Assumptions and Illusions

The path through chaos to a place of thriving will not be without significant challenges. Coping with the social, financial, and environmental challenges will be of paramount importance. However, it is equally important to remember these issues are human-made. Although concrete problems, they spring from within us and our externalized expressions. What drove us to allow such conditions to arise, and what must we change within ourselves to manage the external issues?

To facilitate change, it is extremely important to inquire into how we arrived at our current situation and the way we view ourselves. There is no point in self-recrimination for the problems we have already created. I hope to demonstrate that we as a species are not fatally flawed, but rather, we are the product of the intense process of our relatively recent evolutionary path, which has left us with some significant distortions in our thinking. We need to maintain a healthy self-regard, while making a calm assessment of what impedes us.

Before we can hope to get a large segment of the population to undertake the efforts required to facilitate change, we will need to address our assumptions, illusions, and distractions.

Specifically, the ideas and beliefs about human nature, leadership, and responsibility as they relate to the individual's response to the call for change. If the very human tendency to avoid facing issues directly is not brought into the light, it may well be what pulls us into the darkness. This proclivity is a part of human nature, and we must avoid projecting our collective weaknesses onto a perceived enemy.

This inclination to "enemy making" is one of the mechanisms of the human mind that not only causes us problems but is a huge avoidance of responsibility. It is far better to accept that we have all had a hand in creating our problems. We have a responsibility to ourselves and each other to face the issues. If we take away the judgments we might have about ourselves and other groups or organizations, there is the possibility to look at our strengths and weaknesses as simply the collective challenges and opportunities of our current age. Thus, the looming crisis can be seen as an opportunity to let the self-correcting nature of the universe come into play, as nature seeks to pull systems into a dynamic balance that is inherently somewhat stable. We can use this self-correcting nature to our advantage if we avoid the mistake of the waste and anguish of moral wars on ourselves or each other.

At a time when we are looking at a period of possibly extreme challenge, we will be far better served by having faith in our inner nature and collective capacity. We have met and surpassed all the evolutionary hurdles that have come along so far. Slipping into doubt and imagining a dystopic world of ignorance, brutality, and filth will not support us to do our best in the crisis. I will assess the situation from a more productive and positive perspective with a focus on three levels of human operation: the nature of our species, our Western cultural assumptions, and the individual human response.

THE NATURE OF OUR SPECIES

The question of whether human beings are inherently good or bad has been raised since the birth of Western philosophy, and earlier in Persia. Because we see both good and evil—as we define it—in ourselves, each other, and the world, we feel compelled to resolve the paradox through an answer or story where the apparent dichotomy makes sense. Being brought up in a Western culture, this question was important to me at an early age. After observing the world for a decade and a half, I decided we were on the whole evil, unworthy, and nasty creatures. I held this unhealthy view until I passed through a personal crisis, at which time I reversed that opinion and decided that humankind was essentially good. As I began to mature through the process of personal development, I had a sudden revelation one day—*it does not matter.* The question was not reasonable, and attempts to conclusively resolve the genuine paradox of the human condition are futile. What then to do?

I settled for trying to understand the question as a process; how that process operates in the present and what might be possible in the future. I arrived at what I think is a viable explanation for our behaviour. In very general terms, human beings behave well when they are operating from a place of love and, conversely, behave badly when they are operating from a place of fear. We are not inherently good or bad; we are responding, or reacting, from one or the other of two primary motivators: love or fear. In this sense, love refers to the expansive growth-oriented thrust toward life, while fear refers to the contractive conservative urge to preserve life. In the complex life of a human being, it is common to find both primary motivators are simultaneously at play; there are virtually as many unique expressions of the prime motivators as there are individuals. For instance, the man who deeply loves and protects his family will drop bombs on the family of the hated and feared enemy. This makes the understanding of our motivations very challenging. Unfortunately too few of us spend much time considering what is motivating us, thus sacrificing the freedom and autonomy that comes with conscious choice. This same issue arises at the national level where a country's behaviour is governed by rigid moral tenets, tradition, vanity, or vengeance rather than a compassionate, considered weighing of the possibilities and potential outcomes.

If we can see our behaviour as a choice to operate from either love or fear, we are empowered to manage ourselves in a far more conscious way and are liberated to behave in the world as we ourselves choose. However, this awareness of behavioural choice has not been popular historically. Rather, impulses to opportunism, greed, and cruelty are countered by the social, religious, and ethical imperatives of the time, resulting in the ongoing morality play that underpins much of our culture. The process of putting oneself or one's group on the comfortable side of this split has led to all manner of justifications and rationalizations of beliefs and behaviours.

By pointing at history and "nature," we have managed to justify all sorts of nasty behaviours such as sexism, imperialism, racism, persecution of homosexuals, indifference to the poor, opportunism at all levels, aggression, and war. For a specific example of a historical justification, let us take imperialism. Whether economic or military, it is a process based on the idea that it is appropriate for a society that perceives itself as superior to justify invasion, subjugation, and exploitation of a culture perceived as inferior. When the action is questioned, a common answer is "We humans have always done this; it is just the way of things." There is some truth to this assertion, if we limit our inquiry to a relatively recent historical period. However, this way of doing things has not necessarily always been with us. There is archaeological evidence to suggest that, prior to the Neolithic Revolution, we had more peaceful and egalitarian lives than we have had throughout recorded history. We know from very early recorded history that we have been conquering and enslaving other nations; yet, this is a phenomenon limited to the period of our evolution beginning in the Bronze Age. Thus, we have behaved like this for about 5,000 years out of a total anatomically modern human history of around 200,000 years—a strikingly small percentage.

After the ground-breaking published work of Darwin, some seized on the idea that "survival of the fittest" was the perfect excuse to prey upon and dominate the weak. Further, it has been pointed out that our closest evolutionary relative, the chimpanzee, is often violent, opportunistic, and territorial. This makes for a convenient argument but not a convincing one; equally closely related to us is the bonobo, and its strategy of survival is completely different. Social tensions and opportunities for bonobos are moderated through sexual response rather than violence, and this has proved evolutionarily successful for them.* Nature is not exclusively violent and opportunistic. In fact, modern research has demonstrated that a number of animals will collaborate, show concern for equality, and act compassionately under stress. Such behaviour is not an exclusively primate behaviour but is also seen in other social animals.

Human nature does not stand in the way of our successfully evolving into loving, creative, and sustainable creatures. Yet it does make us susceptible to the opposite. When we have awareness of our human tendencies, behaviour can become a choice. The key is to understand a few critical principles. Many of our unhealthy and unsustainable behaviours stem from maladaptive strategies. These are ancient response processes, which at one time were adaptive strategies that supported our progress but no longer do so. The reason these instincts are now maladaptive is the profound and rapid change of context over the last 5,000 to 8,000 years. The advent of civilization changed what it meant to

---

* For comparative information about behavioural differences between bonobos and chimps, see 3chimps – Hominoid Psychology Research Group, eva.mpg.de/3chimps.

be human, but there has not been sufficient time to significantly change human nature.

Pronatalism, dominance, opportunism, gluttony, hoarding, aggression, cunning, protectiveness, territorialism, and conformity are some of the human characteristics that, in a more ancient context, would have made adaptive sense. For example, opportunism served our species when the opportunities in the environment were much rarer and individual gains contributed to the survival of the tribe through the custom of sharing. If these behaviours were not at one time adaptive, they would never have been part of the human repertoire. With an excess of eight billion people on Earth, characteristics that were adaptive at a time when humans had a small population, primitive technology, and environmental adversity no longer support our survival.

A thoughtful consideration of our motivations would result in a kinder, saner, and more peaceful and sustainable world. The complexity of our thoughts and emotions and the ever-changing situations that we find ourselves in make this a challenging and mutable process; definitive answers as to what is driving us in any given moment may not even be possible. However, it is of great significance to ask the question. Through the process of examining our intentions and motivations, individuals, and ultimately the society we live in, will become a great deal more aware of what we are actually doing and thus empowered to undertake what we really want. The following examples are two ways the human mind organizes itself that have an impact on consciousness.

Projection

In the broadest sense, we project a classification and identity onto anything that we name and form a mental concept of. Identifying, naming, and classifying are the ways we mentally organize our world. Projecting is a basic function of the human mind; it is an unavoidable part of how we think. More specifically, in psychology, projection refers to ascribing certain thoughts, feelings, and behaviours onto others while avoiding accepting those traits within ourselves. These are the disowned parts of the self, the content of our shadow that we cannot allow ourselves to own, although we know on some deep level that they are part of the human experience. And by extension, because we are human, that they are part of us. Therefore, we disown an unacceptable part from our conscious awareness of self and append it to others.

This is not some occasional aberrant behaviour, but rather one that is active in the lives of virtually every human being; it is part of how we establish our identity and a way of being in the world. Unfortunately, it also supports all manner of unhealthy thoughts and deeds, including racism, misogyny, dominance, opportunism, hero worship, and others. The mechanism of projection is almost invariably unconscious. Our projections appear as facts, supporting us to avoid taking personal responsibility and to excuse ourselves of culpability.

Just because projection can support negative behaviours does not mean it is in itself a bad thing; it is simply a part of how we think. Although projection is unconscious and therefore potentially troublesome, it can be brought to a conscious level and the projections withdrawn, thus bringing us to a place of responsibility and a degree of self-mastery that supports us to behave with consciousness.

Myth of Rationality

A rational act is when we carefully consider the reasons before we select a course of action. Humans are capable of rationality, yet we are driven by the non-rational—our impulses, emotions, and needs, both conscious and unconscious. We have the capacity to co-opt our rational minds in the service of the non-rational. It is common to begin with a desire for something and to work to manufacture reasons to justify the pursuit of an action, which is what I call the "myth of rationality." Through the process of rationalization, we develop a mental story that justifies our behaviours as reasonable, necessary, or even noble, in order to do what we want.

It is exceedingly common for people to be unconscious of the misuse of reason and to believe their own self-justifications regardless of how objective reasoning might assess the situation. This is how people can go about doing selfish and unpleasant things and still feel good about themselves. The use of rationalization is not inherently wrong. Rather, it is how it is consciously used that matters. If we can accept that many of our needs and desires are non-rational yet valid, we can own them without self-reproach or see them for what they are in circumstances where they might be harmful. Through this we would learn something about ourselves, become more responsible, and gain a greater degree of self-mastery. The key is to apply conscious compassion rather than self-justification through the myth of rationality.

THE WESTERN CULTURAL CONTEXT

One of the peculiar and persistent quirks of civilized human beings is that we often look outside ourselves for a source of solutions to our problems. This is a product of civilization, wherein millennia of hierarchy, state religion, superstition, and associative thinking have impressed upon us that something or someone out there will handle the issues for us. In the face of an epochal shift whose successful outcome will require a profound change in human behaviour and participation of a large segment of the population, the ideas of external rescue or that the great problems are somebody else's responsibility are dangerous ones. The danger lies in our abdication of responsibility and the willingness to let someone, or something, manage the outcome. This dynamic has been exacerbated by the ever-increasing complexity of our society, where complex infrastructure, legal systems, and sheer size have made it harder for anyone to become an effective member.

Staying small and ignoring the issues is by no means a universal response. There are caring and effective people who have taken on some of the challenges, and their numbers appear to be increasing. Unfortunately, however, the majority are not engaged in the work of healthy change, and I do not believe we will manage an epochal shift through a small minority of the population. A minority might lead, but ultimately, for an evolutionary leap, a significant majority is required.

The second issue is how to institute change. Working through established systems is unlikely to yield success, because our institutions have played a large role in creating the problems in the first place. Working within the existing systems might have some effect over time; however, the opportunistic, adversarial thinking that created them remains the same. The answer rests with evolution—personal evolution. We are the building blocks of the systems we use, and only when enough of us have evolved will it be possible to change the systems to ultimately create a new order of human organization. I believe this is the only way we can create sufficient change within a reasonable time frame to meet the critical issues we are facing.

An overview follows of three of the systems that need to be addressed, why we have put our faith in these systems, how they self-perpetuate, and the magnitude of the task of changing them.

Science

The scientific method is an unsurpassed tool for exploring the physical world. There is no doubt about its positive contribution to our lives. It is one of the finest achievements of the human mind, and it underpins many of our great advancements. Science changes our world, but it has had little effect on our motivations, attitudes, or other aspects of our interior process. It has given us the longest, healthiest, and most affluent lifestyles ever enjoyed. However, it has also given us high-tech weapons of destruction and has facilitated the cycle of production, consumption, and disposal that is depleting our resources and polluting our earth.

As long as we are driven by archaic motivations that we don't understand, the outcomes of science will reflect this drive. To bring the full might of science to our aid, we need to develop our consciousness and compassion to the point where we can draw on science to bring forth truly adaptive strategies. When this happens, we will have unleashed one of the greatest powers at our disposal to mitigate the formidable problems facing our species.

Scientific research is an expensive pursuit that requires lengthy, sophisticated training and often significant facilities, materials, and equipment. Much research funding is controlled by those who have a vested interest in particular outcomes. In a nutshell, the issue can be summarized in the old jest. *Remember the golden rule: whoever has the gold rules.* Serious science reviewers have pointed to the practice of contracting out research to non-academic research groups, undisclosed conflicts of interest, and pressure to please funding bodies as factors that taint scientific objectivity. This phenomenon is not limited to private sector funding; a Wikipedia entry on Funding of Science cites a 2005 study in the journal *Nature* that surveyed 3,247 US researchers who were funded by the National Institutes of Health. The survey showed that 15.5 percent of the scientists questioned "admitted to altering design, methodology, or results of their studies due to pressure of an external funding source."

The issue is two-fold: the objectivity of science is at risk, and the direction in which scientific efforts are being pushed is currently driven by economic, military, and special interest funding.

For research to be directed toward solving global issues, there must be a will to take them on. Science is a powerful and effective tool if applied and focused in an appropriate direction. But we cannot sit and wait for science and technology to rescue us. We must take individual responsibility to push for scientific pursuits that serve humanity and the environment. A delicate balance must be struck that maintains the intellectual freedom and spirit of exploration essential to good science while, at the same time, directing science toward the general benefit of creating a more sustainable world.

Leadership
There is a pervasive belief in our culture that any grouping of people must have a single, prominent person leading that group if the group is to be effective. From the dawn of civilization until relatively recent times, this figure has almost invariably been male and has been referred to by the scholars of prehistory as "the big man."* Alternatively referred to as an "aggrandizer," this role arose in the period between the adaptation of agriculture and the social organization of the Bronze Age. These were men whose energy, opportunism, and drive to dominate ran higher than that of their peers at a time when the social and economic situation enabled it to make a real difference. Before the agricultural revolution and the adaptation of sedentary lifestyles, the opportunity of such men to express their dominance was muted by the social milieu, mobility, and hunter-gatherer economics. Specifically, such attributes as high energy, opportunism, and aggression would be aimed at the service of the tribe, and there was little that could be accumulated and kept for oneself. It was likely a very communal life with opportunities to exhibit leadership limited in scope, duration, and reward, which all served the collective group.

However, with the coming of agriculture, our individual abilities and instincts could be turned to another use. Surplus

---

* This is distinct from the contemporary, relatively egalitarian Big Man leadership pattern in Melanesian societies of the South Pacific where leaders use persuasion and wisdom to exercise influence even if they do not have formal authority. (See wikipedia.org/wiki/Big_man_(anthropology).)

production allowed acquisition of resources, which in turn allowed us to pursue self-interest. One of the chief methods of advancing self-interest and gaining prestige in early agrarian cultures was through feasting. Certainly, feasting was far older than agriculture, but pre-agriculture feasting would have been tied to serendipitous highly successful hunts or the seasonal availability of a surplus of fruits, fish, or game. With the ability to consolidate and hold resources, such as grain or livestock, the situation changed. Feasts in this new context could be used to gain significant social and material advantage.

In his book *The Uniqueness of Western Civilization*, Ricardo Duchesne states: "The power came from the creation of social debt among the people attending the feast. The aggrandizer, by redistributing his own resources to the attendees at the feast, many of whom did not have the means to reciprocate in kind, was able to expand the number of people who were in an asymmetrical relationship to him" (p. 383). Beneficiaries were indebted with a debt they could not pay; this brought people into an unequal social relationship. Though the big man might not have gained economically, he would gain in prestige and social opportunities. In tight-knit communities, this prestige could be a significant benefit. The attendees of such feasts, though socially indebted, would gain some degree of support and possibly protection from the big man.

There were risks involved in putting forward much of one's accumulated wealth—risks commensurate with potential gains and therefore worth taking. Again from Duchesne: "The important point is that successful feasters did enjoy the biggest families, the ability to broker the best bride, the most domestic animals, the best land, and the most prestigious trade goods" (p. 383). The great game of materialism had begun, and a class of people had arisen who were determined to win it. Along with the material gains and the emotional perks of prestige came the very real power of being the big man in a village. Ultimately, people would come to such a man to settle disputes, seek advice, and plead for various kinds of support and protection.

As societies became more complex and stratified, the role of the big man eventually evolved into that of the headman. The role of the headman shifted significantly when those men were powerful enough to take and enforce their hereditary position in society rather than being chosen. These headmen collectively formed what can be considered an elite, which was in turn supported by each of the chief's retainers, advisers, and principal warriors. Society was further stratified and rigid structures began to form, giving the society stability and ensuring the advantage of the headman and his cadre.

This was the level of social development of the Proto-Indo-European peoples who came in waves from the Pontic Steppes between 4200 and 2200 BCE to change the face of Europe forever. They were a pastoral and heroic people. Heroic in this sense refers to the style of chieftainship, a warrior cult of opportunism based on the control of trade, raiding, and wars of conquest. The social and economic base was in the pastoral holdings of the lower class, while the controlling class was that of glory-seeking opportunists. The upper class structured society, offered protection, and brought wealth. They became individuals that people learned to revere. With the continuing evolution of society, some of the headmen became kings, forming an aristocracy with their relatives and retainers as the nobility of the land.

Slowly, in different centres of civilization across the globe, humans began to write. One of the first non-economic uses of writing was to record the lineage, glories, and exploits of kings and emperors. Thus, history was born. Writing preserved the identity of ancient leaders by recording their prowess and wealth, their constructed facilities and monuments, those they conquered, and the empires they built. It was all about the leaders. Little of the toils, suffering, and contributions of the common people were recorded. The historical writing and reciting of the leaders were other ways they impressed their essential importance upon the commoners to gain their unquestionable right to rule. The great significance and appropriateness of the leader was often supplemented by a mutually supportive allegiance with their spiritual counterparts in the priesthood and/or some kind of claim to divine origin for themselves. Every step of the way, the common people were shown that only through the great leader's protection, generosity, wisdom, and divinity might safety and prosperity become reasonably assured. When the commoners accepted the system, they could become physically and psychologically dependent on it.

This was the way of things through the period of great empire building into the Iron Age. For the West, the Greek Empire laid down by Alexander set the template, followed by the mighty Roman Empire. This system came crashing down in the 5th century CE, bringing an end to the era of highly centralized domination by a faraway emperor. Europe was left to its own devices. Gradually, order emerged out of the chaos, and not surprisingly, it was based on the concept of leadership by a single dominant male and his various ranks of retainers. The feudal system and Catholic Church emerged, two structures that would continue to support supremacy of the patriarchy for many centuries.

Throughout centuries there were occasional uprisings and riots to protest the social system; the peasant revolts were often ruthlessly repressed. Significant social change was not witnessed until the Renaissance. With the dawn of early modern science in the latter part of that period, along with the development of an independent middle class and the spread of literacy, age-old assumptions began to be cast into serious doubt. With the era of the Enlightenment, people began to consider philosophies in which the church, and historic power structures, were questioned and sometimes abandoned. The assumption of the birthright to govern was severely questioned, giving rise to the ideas and eventual success of democratic models. As the power and prestige of the church, royalty, and nobility were curtailed, individuals who sought power and prestige adapted to the development of new models for the self-aggrandizer.

As Western culture emerged into the modern era, the role of organized religion in the power dynamics of a temporal society fell significantly. Religion retained power where that power was based on the individual's affections. The monarchies suffered a similar fate, as they were gradually relegated to figureheads or eliminated altogether. In this societal restructuring, the need for societal order was not reduced but simply redirected into new structures. Those structures were centred on "great men" and generally coalesced into two main categories: political and corporate.

There have been numerous examples throughout history of rare and notable leaders who have operated principally for a greater good. Commonly, however, leaders have been motivated by the opportunity for wealth, power, and prestige. Ancient history suggests these were the original motives for leadership.

The need for power and prestige is a compensation for a lack of love, one of the primary universal human needs. Achieving power and prestige temporarily fills that void, yet never satisfies it. This is the same mechanism that drives most, if not all, addictive-compulsive behaviours—a deep need that is not met but merely satiated in the moment by a substitution, which sets up the classic addiction cycle that drives the individual to maintain or increase the supply of the substitution. This opens the conventional leadership model to potential abuses of power. These people will misbehave for the same reasons someone with a serious substance issue does—they need their fix.

In order for a situation to become sane and sustainable over time, authority must be equally balanced with responsibility. To put a person in a place of responsibility without commensurate authority is to make a slave or martyr of them. Such a person bears the weight of the outcome without the means to affect the process leading to that outcome. Conversely, if a person is given authority without responsibility, this puts them in a position to become a tyrant or abusive opportunist. Without responsibility for the outcome, having the authority to act means an individual can do as they please with disregard for how it affects others, the economy, environment, or other systems. The checks and balances that result from coupling responsibility to authority reduce the likelihood of power abuse and increase the probability of the results serving the greater good.

The adversarial system, which rewards those who dominate their peers, has only been with us since the rise of civilization. Previously, the cultural assumption had been that we must collaborate to ensure the tribe is healthy and supports us. But civilization, and the gradual stratification of society, had a profound effect on our culture and thinking. In its crudest form, the adversarial system sorts for the most aggressive, avaricious, and self-centred individual. Though it is rarely expressed so crudely in modern culture, most of the competition for position is tinged to varying degrees with those characteristics.

There are numerous societal problems created by the adversarial system, most of which are offshoots of the polarization and separation that adversarial behaviours foment. By separating two or more rival persons, ideologies, religions, policies, or whatever, we make the unselected element unworthy and dismiss it. This means there are winners and losers, bad ideas and good ideas, people who are right and people who are wrong, black and white. This is the principle that underlies enemy making, militant morality, intolerance, and bigotry.

Perhaps from the perspective of our evolution, one of the most serious impacts on our species is the development and persistence of an infantile mindset, which involves the willingness to remain compliant, conformist, and obedient to those in charge. Being infantile makes us susceptible to the potential of having our maladaptive instincts manipulated by our leaders' self-interest. We can be induced to have certain beliefs, behave in specific ways, and offer support to dangerous ideas. Simply put, we can be manipulated to ignore serious problems on the social, economic, and environmental fronts and to support flagrant materialism, prejudice, and war. By allowing ourselves to be too easily led, we step back from personal responsibility and do not think for ourselves, an essential component of genuine democracy. If we are forever bound by rules made by others, we lose the faculty of ethical decision-making and the importance of taking responsibility for those decisions.

In addition, various cultural advances have made conventional leadership somewhat redundant, perpetuated by habits of mind and tradition rather than on its merits. One of the major factors in this regard is the higher level of education and awareness of the general population. Before the 1800s, education was limited to upper-class males. This set up a situation where they would quite naturally be the individuals most likely equipped to step into positions of power. However, following that era there was an expansion of general education which, as the National Institute of Economic and Social Research discussion paper "Education and Economic Growth" (Philip Stevens and Martin Weale, 2003) explains, largely happened in the past two hundred years. "In the United Kingdom elementary education did not become compulsory until 1870. Very limited free secondary education was introduced in 1907 and it was not until 1944 that universal free secondary education was introduced. Only a small minority benefited from tertiary education until almost the end of the twentieth century."

The last major revision of our democratic process took place at the beginning of the period of generalized education. This revision was catalyzed by the revolutions in France and America, which prompted reforms in many other nations. It is not surprising that the methods of democracy reflected the social structure of the times. The people who could vote were deemed to be the people who could be expected to have enough education to make informed decisions. At that time, this meant the wealthier (usually land-owning) male members of society. The criteria shifted over the intervening period, most notably by the inclusion of women in voting populations; however, the basic structure remained the same. For the majority of the population, the contribution to important decisions was a single ballot cast every three or four years, limited to supporting a leader and their ideologies. The big men still called the shots, with relative independence from the input of the general population. This may have been an appropriate way to structure things in 1800 CE, but it should now be passé. The current population is generally educated, with easy access to information and resources, and quite capable of making sound, informed decisions.

Factors other than conventional education have made our populations more sophisticated. It would be difficult to calculate the positive effects of the cross-cultural exchange of ideas, methods, and practices such as Eastern meditation, yoga, art, literature, and philosophy, but I believe they are immense. In addition, the ongoing advances of science are largely available to any interested individual. In light of all this, we need to make significant changes to patterns of leadership that reflect the changes in the social fabric by increasing our participation in decision-making and deepening democracy.

The human propensity for collaboration gives us an alternative to conventional leadership. Members of our genus were likely inclined to collaborate when we were tree dwellers. When we became ground-dwelling animals, we had to face serious threats, and the odds of surviving the advances of a large predator went up with the number of spears you could face it with. This was also the case as we progressed to hunting the great beasts of the era, like mammoth, giant elk, and aurochs. How much better were our odds of success if undertaken in a group—better yet, an organized group with a plan of how we defend ourselves or hunt? There would have been multiple survival benefits to collaboration, and these would have been enhanced through the ages by our developing brains and the refinement of language. This is how we survived and thrived, not because we have powerful jaws, great speed, or massive strength, but because we are clever, we can communicate, and we collaborate.

This state of affairs shifted with the material and social changes that came out of the Neolithic Revolution and the rise of the big man. After thousands of years of dominance-based autocratic rule, we have largely put aside collaboration in favour of hierarchy. Most people have mistakenly come to see this as the natural order, believing that safety, prosperity, and all good things come from strong leadership, and that leadership must come from a special individual, one who is rich, popular, or powerful. Alternative forms of leadership, particularly leadership based on the wisdom of a larger collective, tend to be overlooked or dismissed.

I believe humans have a natural impulse toward spirituality, a desire to understand the great and mysterious questions of life. One can deny mystery and attempt to explain all elements of existence in reductionist/materialist terms, or one can embrace the assumption that there are, in the universe, forces beyond ourselves that govern the nature of things. As people with the latter perspective form a significant majority of the population, they look for information, inspiration, and guidance in spiritual matters. Whether they seek their own personal understanding or align with long-established religious institutions, there is an obvious need for spiritual leadership in our society.

Spiritual leadership can fall prey to many of the same weaknesses as conventional leadership can; however, there are also other unique challenges. To reach, teach, and manage a large religious body generally requires simplifying the message, strictly codifying it, and introducing a class of special administrators. The results are dogma and religious hierarchy, which obscure the call to spiritual growth in favour of conformity. This rigidifying reduces practices that were originally intended to support growth to a ritual form designed to maintain membership and achieve salvation.

A highly structured spiritual system can offer social connection, a sense of belonging, a chance to contribute, and most of all, relief from the terrible uncertainty around mortality and the afterlife. While these are beneficial outcomes, they generally come with the risk of dependency rather than growth and little or no direct access to spiritual experience or personal interpretation of such experience if it happens. All of that is mediated by an appointed leader or functionary of some kind, focused on explaining and maintaining the "one true path" they espouse. Rather than facilitating the personal spiritual growth of the individual, the impetus is to narrow the possible range of experience and investigation in order to contain it. I believe the point of spiritual leadership is to support individuals to directly experience, interpret, and integrate their spiritual awareness—to evoke the light within us. Spiritual leaders can be of considerable support to ground us in our spirituality and thus assist us to be of greater service to our species and our world.

Accessing the wisdom of the group and converging ideas into a clear decision take a special form of leadership, referred to by some as the servant leader model. This model can be understood by looking at three of its distinctive elements: objectives, method, and source of power. The objectives are focused on achieving the best decision for all concerned in a given situation. The methods used to achieve the end result are quite different from a hierarchical structure, because the only way anyone can know what is best for the group is by involving the group in the decision. Servant leaders facilitate the discussion, support the group to co-create the plan or decision, guide its implementation, and share responsibility for the results. Their power is in direct relation to their ability to serve. They act as a focus for the energy and initiative, not as its source.

This type of leadership centres around relationship skills: the ability to communicate, maintain an open mind and heart, and manage personal and group boundaries. Although there may be some situations where this type of leadership would not be appropriate, transforming conventional leadership to a lateral organizational structure would support a broader base of participation and a governance system where the interests of future generations are more likely to be considered, resulting in a more sustainable world.

Current cultural attitudes and beliefs are the only real impediment to collaboration. We are so inured to the relative comfort of the current social structure, where others make decisions for us, that it is hard to imagine the degree of freedom, authority, and self-responsibility we could realize under a new leadership regime. A shift in leadership is an essential ingredient of the restructuring required to support a sustainable future.

Revolution
A revolutionary movement occurs when a group rebels against an authoritarian structure they believe is oppressing them in some way. These situations are usually charged with great passion that has arisen from the length and severity of the oppression. When this passion for change meets the resistance of the status quo, there

is conflict that ranges from legal contests to war. It is an expensive process that destabilizes infrastructures, wastes resources, causes suffering, and costs lives. War has limited use in bringing lasting positive change to the human condition.

Whichever side you are on, whether you perceive your side to have won or lost, you still lose. The psychic scars on the people on both sides set the stage for the whole terrible sequence to happen again. If we look at some of the well-known revolutions of recent history, we begin to see a disturbing cycle. For example, in 1917 the Bolshevik revolutionaries in Russia overthrew their Czarist oppressors and began a new state, one for the people. However, twenty years later the situation had gotten a little ugly: Joseph Stalin orchestrated the Great Purge, a large-scale campaign of repression and murder, from 1936 to 1938. He cleared out Communist Party and government officials as well as the Red Army leadership, repressed the peasant class, and persecuted members of the public identified as "saboteurs," using police surveillance, imprisonment, and arbitrary executions. Ironically the rebels had taken on the qualities of the status quo they had overthrown.

This pattern shows up to some degree in the histories of all revolutions. They start by responding to a genuine problem of oppression. Assuming they succeed, they build a new and more idealistic institution. This institution becomes the new status quo and starts to "protect" its survival through various forms of control and repression. Although circumstances will have changed, possibly improving, we have come back to the same problem—the abuse of power. Such cycles of revolution have a huge cost and make only minimal progress.

The real problem that revolutions set out to rectify is the abuse of power, but the mistaken belief is that the entrenched status quo is the oppressor. Rulers who have unrestricted power and minimal responsibility will likely misbehave, sometimes very badly.

The issue is power and leadership. The oppression itself is merely a symptom; the circumstances of the oppression are merely one particular iteration of the problem of unbridled leadership. It is certainly understandable that a group would want to shake off the oppression, but unfortunately, even if they succeed, they will only temporarily drive the problem underground. Sadly, as we have seen, it is often a later generation of the recently liberated rebels who become the next iteration of oppressors.

Addressing the abuse of power will require a collective change in how we see and relate to these issues. We need to make our relationship to power conscious: to examine it with ruthless honesty, decide on an appropriate response, and then put our energy into cultivating power within ourselves. That is where a new relationship to power must start. Once enough of us have moved out of our denial and achieved a healthy, positive relationship to power, then a new dynamic will begin to appear. As the standards shift on the grassroots level, they will inevitably put pressure on our existing systems to change along with them. If this process is successful, we will have achieved an evolution rather than relying on revolution to facilitate change.

Rebellions are another facet of the adversarial system and the failure of dominance-based leadership. As we reassess this issue, the new processes that emerge will be able to draw on two major sources: fresh creative innovation and our ancient fundamental nature as collaborators. The synthesis of these elements and the demands of the time will shape leadership and social structures in the future. In small ways, this change is already beginning. Although far from mainstream, an increasing number of organizations are using alternative approaches and gaining skills and experience with these methods. The way of the future is already beginning to show itself.

THE INDIVIDUAL HUMAN RESPONSE

There are basically two directions that humans can go under duress: come together for mutual support, or degenerate into predatory opportunism. To a large extent, the direction is governed by how we handle our fears. If we follow the idea that "There ain't much left, and I'm gettin' mine now," we stand the chance of creating something like the dystopian post-apocalyptic worlds so popular in Hollywood films. On the other hand, if we can manage our fears, maintain our composure, and pursue self-responsibility and collaboration, we could get a very different result. Granted, we could not control the material problems completely, but with the collective effort of a group of mature people of goodwill, we could guide the situation in the best way for all concerned. This is an important factor to consider even before things get difficult: How do I intend to deal with my fears, losses, and shifts in fortune? What are the most loving and creative responses I could have?

One of the first things we may want to consider is whether to choose a radical or conservative approach to problem solving. It is common for people to identify with one end or the other of the spectrum, often with increasing polarization as the stress increases. In so many human endeavours, we can currently see a deepening rift between left and right perspectives, environmentalists and resource extractors, traditionalists and innovators. The continuum of choice between radical and conservative has been a natural part of how human cultures have maintained a dynamic balance—weighing the urge to run off in new directions against the desire to conserve what we already have. Both approaches are necessary to stable human progress under normal societal conditions. However, as we approach a critical transitional period, we must recognize that conditions are no longer normal.

The old ways that have traditionally worked for us are failing and must be modified into—or replaced by—new methods, systems, and structures. At the same time, we cannot afford to go grasping after straws in an ungrounded attempt to find new solutions. We need to respect both the constrictive forces that seek stability and the expansive forces that seek change, and apply them with care and consciousness to the current situation. This, however, becomes more and more difficult as our fears increase and the perceived gulf between conservatism and radicalism widens. In such circumstances, there is a tendency to abandon objective middle-of-the-road thinking and move into the camp of one or the other of the two polarities. This brings up the significant danger, clearly apparent today, of enemy making, scapegoating, and polarized judgment. When these attitudes arise, we lose objectivity and sink back into the wasteful, destructive ways of the adversarial system. In such a scenario, creativity and energy is channelled as much into winning as it is into problem solving. There is a seductive quality to this tendency that draws on distorted elements of our ancient nature.

It therefore becomes immensely important for us to be aware of the possibility of being pulled into competition when what we really need is co-creativity. Assuming we are truly committed to a loving and sustainable world, we cannot afford the waste of energy, resources, and time or the separation this polarity can create. Awareness, curiosity, open-mindedness, and compassion must be continuously cultivated as we move forward.

This asks a great deal of us as seekers and servant leaders. It is no small task to hold a compassionate, balanced stance while staying consistently focused on the greater objective in the midst of passions—our own and those of others. We need to do more than develop self-awareness and compassion. We must also cultivate our courage and crystallize our resolve to the highest possible degree, ideally, to bring a nobility to our purpose that transcends the more common passion of commitment to a cause. We need to hold ourselves as in our best ideal of the ancient archetype of the Knight, keeping our hearts and minds in their most open, healthy states, while relentlessly moving forward. No small task indeed, but hopefully an inspiring one.

Can we do this? Facing the inevitable intersection of the doom curves of declining resources, burgeoning population, increasing environmental degradation, and so forth, can we expect our species to make a leap forward? Especially when we are mired in a context of unenlightened self-interest, adversarialism, fear, and complexity? If we lose ourselves dwelling on this sort of speculation, we rob ourselves of vital energy and decimate our resolve.

One source of a wider perspective can be found in nature. One such beautiful and fitting example was offered to me by author and public speaker Anodea Judith (anodeajudith.com). It is the analogy of the butterfly. As we know, the butterfly is the last stage of the complex life cycle of the creature that begins as an egg and hatches into a larva or caterpillar. During the larval stage, the caterpillar is a voracious feeder, constantly consuming all the palatable resources it can reach. Through the process of constant ingestion and conversion of food, the caterpillar grows large and fat and, after a certain point, begins its pupal stage. Generally, the creature stops eating now and focuses on building a cocoon to house itself during the amazing process of metamorphosis. It is in this stage that the magic transformation from a fat caterpillar to a colourful butterfly takes place, and this is where it gets truly interesting for us.

Though the creature now makes no gross physical movements, things are on the move within it. Miraculously, specialized cells are beginning to form within the tissues of the pupa. These cells go by the intriguing name of imaginal cells, presumably because they are "imagining" the beginnings of a butterfly. These cells are different, being essentially butterfly cells, not caterpillar cells, and the pupa's immune system attacks them. However, once started, the process cannot be halted, and more imaginal cells form and begin to connect to others. The individuals and then the groups grow and strengthen until they become the dominant modality within the creature. At this point, the imaginal cells draw on the energy stored in the remaining caterpillar cells to complete the transformation. All that remains is for the new creature to fight its way clear of the debris of the now unnecessary cocoon, emerge, and spread its wings.

Judith points out how much the life cycle of a single creature can be a metaphor for the evolution of our species. For thousands of years, humanity has been on the increase, consuming an ever-larger volume of the available resources, and in fact, getting ever better at resource extraction and use. Through this process we have grown "fat," and like the caterpillar, torpor has set in on our collective culture. Encased in our own materialism, we are on the cusp of profound change—an internal change. We can see the emergence of the seeker / servant leader, just as we saw the emergence of the imaginal cells in the insect. This is our moment; the culture is frozen externally in its same old behaviours, and we are the beginning of its internal change. What remains is for our loving creative being to call others to the awakening. When enough come online, then it is just a matter of time until our chief tasks will be to dig ourselves out of the relics of the old culture and spread our wings.

We cannot be sure that this will be the trajectory our species will take, but the parallels are quite striking. Further, it is unlikely that nature or the divine (however you view it) would have set us up for failure. In other words, I believe the potential to survive the crisis and eventually thrive is innate in our species' template. In our rising from obscurity to become the dominant species, an amazing amount of the planet's available resources have been consumed, and I think this investment was not made lightly. We are by no means guaranteed success, but it seems weighted that way. The task now is to have faith, play our part, resist the "immune system" of our degenerating culture, and awaken the latent powers within to become the imaginal cells of our species.

So I think we should not despair or feel overwhelmed. The outcome for our species will be decided by forces much larger and more complex than us. In the end, I believe we have a slightly better than even chance of species survival and a 100 percent chance of personally contributing meaningfully to a positive outcome if we have the heart and will for it.

One of the demons that can undermine our capacity to serve joyously is the insidious presence of self-doubt. *Am I good enough, am I worthy of this cause, am I smart enough?* These are the reverberations of old voices from the lessons of our childhoods, designed to save us from the sins of vanity and grandiosity. For many of us, these well-meaning messages were overplayed to the point of leaving us with a lasting liability. Usually, the amplitude of these messages fades through the awakening processes of personal development.

Personal growth, personal challenges, and global change will inevitably bring us up against realities we do not like. In fact, for many of us, the state of the environment and the suffering of our fellow human beings is a cause for anguish, despair, and depression. When we feel depressed, overwhelmed, and hopeless, our effectiveness is dramatically reduced, putting us in danger of becoming part of the problem rather than part of the solution. We need to take care of our own needs in a healthy way. Enjoying humour and celebration and receiving support from compassionate, like-minded people who share our objectives builds our energy, commitment, and above all resilience, which is essential to face what is coming our way.

Chapter Three

Being Human

THE FACTS WE (ALMOST) KNOW

We cannot know what we are and where we are capable of going unless we know what we were and where we came from. However, the exploration and analysis of our prehistoric past is inherently difficult and a thorough investigation of prehistory is far beyond the scope of this book. The objective here is simply to develop a broad general understanding of our origins.

There are challenges to the study of our origins in prehistory. We have soft bodies that do not preserve well, and early on, there were not that many of us. Compared to those of the ancient mollusks whose hard bodies and high populations have left massive, preserved deposits for study, finds of human and pre-human fossils are rare and precious. When human fossils and associated artifacts are found, the nature of a whole species may be inferred from a handful of samples. This is difficult for even the most scrupulous scientist, and at times it brings those scientists into contention, leading to conclusions that are uncertain. In addition, new fossil finds and assessment technologies change our ideas, models, and terminology. An example is the amazing discovery of a new human species, the Denisovans, whose existence was established by the study of a single fossilized finger bone found in 2010 using analysis of mitochondrial DNA. Given the investigative complexity, I have done my best to navigate and establish a simplified general outline.

We view ourselves as a clever and classy unique species, yet we are nonetheless the progeny of the great old-world apes. What is known as the "superfamily" of the great apes has evolved through numerous genera. In the murky depths of time between 12 and 7 million years ago, our species evolved as a divergence from the other great apes. We split off from the common ancestral group that gave rise to us and our nearest cousins, the chimpanzees. The distinguishing feature is the adaptation to a fully bipedal stance. Over a great passage of time, this key feature brought about a series of adaptive changes to human anatomy and behaviour that would yield our species as we know it today.

There were several stages to that evolutionary process, through the long and uncertain era of the transitional species. A number of fossil finds from northeast Africa sparked claims of the first bipedals, yet a clear lineage and the assignment of a genus name remains beyond our reach. It is sufficient to say that at least one line of this group managed to achieve fully erect posture and catalyzed an amazing evolutionary journey.

The following is a generalized outline of our evolutionary path; I have chosen not to address the numerous controversies surrounding nearly every step of that evolution.

The Australopithecines

Although our understanding of the very early situation remains complex and shifting, by approximately 3.5 million years ago we seem to be on firmer ground with the categorization of the genus Australopithecus. We now have clear evidence that there were successful bipedal predecessors to our line living in Africa.

Most Australopithecus were relatively small and slender, standing between 3 foot 11 and 4 foot 7. There is a notable difference in size between the sexes, with the male being significantly taller. Their brain size is approximately 35 percent that of modern humans, roughly equivalent to a modern ape's. It is generally thought that Australopithecus used tools no more than the great apes of today; they would not have produced tools for a future use and retained them.

Homo habilis
By around 2.4 million years ago, a new species of creature had evolved that is generally considered the first of the genus Homo. These creatures were the Homo habilis (extinct circa 1.4 million years ago). They had significantly larger brain capacity than the Australopithecines, approximately half that of an average modern human. Brain capacity, a reduction in the protruding profile of the face, and associated stone tools are considered justification for classification of fossil remains in the genus Homo. Their tools were in what is called the Oldowan style: simple, rough, and not particularly symmetrical. My personal experience with picking up and handling some of these simple tools at the University of British Columbia Museum of Anthropology, and feeling how well they fit in my hand, has firmly anchored in my mind that the tool maker was undoubtedly human.

Homo erectus (ergaster)
The fossil evidence of Homo erectus ranges from 1.9 million to 143,000 years ago. Homo erectus follows the same trend as it differentiates itself from habilis as habilis did from the Australopithecines, namely, an increase in cranial volume, a flatter face, and reduced brow ridges. The cranial capacity ranges from 850 to 1,100 cc, bringing erectus into the low end of the range of modern humans. H. erectus was a slender creature and fairly tall, up to 5 foot 10 for males. Sexual dimorphism could see the females as much as 25 percent smaller than males.

H. erectus appears to have begun with a similar technology as its predecessor habilis, namely the simple Oldowan. However, the African population of erectus went on to develop a new and more sophisticated stone technology known as the Acheulean at around 1.8 million years ago. These stone tools were characterized by distinctive oval and pear-shaped "hand axes"; studies of surface-wear patterns reveal their uses included butchering and skinning game, digging soil, and cutting wood or other plant materials. Another critically important technology that erectus seems to have achieved was the harnessing of fire, perhaps as far back as 1 million years ago, although it is unclear to what extent erectus cooked their food. It is also thought that erectus may have been the first Homo species to have invented rafts.

H. erectus was probably the first hominid to live in small familial groups similar to modern hunter-gatherer band societies. They were also thought to be the first hominid to hunt in coordinated groups and use complex tools. They are believed to have cared for their infirm and aged. Evidence suggests that they were likely capable of modern speech. Taken together, these elements can be seen as a major movement toward modern behaviours.

Homo heidelbergensis

Homo heidelbergensis is an extinct species of the genus Homo that lived in Africa, Europe, and western Asia from at least 600,000 years ago and may date back 1,300,000 years. H. heidelbergensis survived until about 250,000 to 200,000 years ago. Heidelbergensis's distinction from its predecessor erectus is a larger brain case, with a volume of between 1,100 to 1,400 cc, which overlaps the modern human average of 1,350 cc. With height and weight coming in at 5 foot 9 and 136 pounds for males and 5 foot 2 and 112 pounds for females, these beings were of a similar size to their predecessor, H. erectus.

H. heidelbergensis seems to have inherited the Acheulean stone technology of erectus. However, there is evidence that at least some groups made stone-tipped hunting spears. Later species, H. neanderthalensis and H. sapiens, may have inherited the use of the spear from them. Also, heidelbergensis almost certainly had controlled use of fire, but it is uncertain if they used it to cook their food.

H. heidelbergensis would also have had the capacity for speech and would have further refined the ability. The morphology of the inner and outer ear support heidelbergensis's ability to hear a wide range of sounds similar to the range of modern humans. It seems likely that the development of language and culture would go hand in hand, and it has been suggested that in this case, development went as far as simple symbolic thinking and early use of ritual.

An important feature about H. heidelbergensis is that this species is believed to have given rise to three other species: Neanderthals, Denisovans, and modern humans (Homo sapiens).

Homo neanderthalensis
The Neanderthals were a stocky, sturdy folk with average heights and weights coming in at 5 foot 6 and 170 pounds for males and 5 foot 1 and 146 pounds for females. Their skeletal structure indicates they were more heavily muscled and stronger than their early modern human counterparts. Notable also are the shortness of limbs, barrel chest, heavy brow ridges, and facial protrusion in comparison to early modern humans.

As well as the heavy brows, the nose was longer and broader and started higher on the face. Neanderthals had an average cranial capacity of 1,600 cc, which is notably greater than our present modern average of 1,350 cc.

Neanderthals used and advanced a stone tool technology called the Mousterian, notably creating much more precise and light tools than their predecessors. They made a wide range of tools, including quartz hand axes, three-sided picks, points, and stone cleavers. It is also thought that they moved beyond the raft for water crossing, having developed the dugout canoe. There is evidence that Neanderthals, in some regions, built dwellings of a long-lasting nature.

Though relying heavily on meat, the Neanderthals also ate plant products, and they cooked their food. They made jewellery and possibly symbolic art. They cared for their aged and infirm and did intentional burial. These were no shuffling ape-men; rather, people much like us. And of course, with conclusive proof of interbreeding between Neanderthals and Homo sapiens, there can be no doubt that they were of the same species as us. This is based on Ernst Mayr's definition of species (in his 1996 *Philosophy of Science* article "What is a species and what is not?"), namely: "Species are groups of interbreeding natural populations that are reproductively isolated from other such groups."

The Denisovans

Along with their cousins, the Neanderthals, the Denisovans are believed to have speciated away from the same common ancestor, H. heidelbergensis, about 600,000 years ago. They then split again from their sister group, the Neanderthals, about 200,000 years later, presumably in the area of the Middle East. From there they appear to have struck off east and north. They also bred with H. sapiens, resulting in 3 to 5 percent of Denisovan DNA in Micronesians and Australian Aborigines. Due to their very recent discovery (2010) and the very limited finds (one finger bone, one toe bone, and two teeth), very little is known about the Denisovans other than their genome.

Others

Homo floresiensis is the proposed classification of a group of hominids found on the island of Flores in Indonesia in 2003. Controversy rages about whether these beings can be considered in the genus Homo. In 1979 in China, the remains of unusual hominids were found that have a rather strange mix of modern and archaic human characteristics. The remains have been carbon dated to between 14,500 and 11,500 years of age. While they are considered Homo, their sub-species is unclear; perhaps it is their own.

A HISTORICAL OVERVIEW

Anatomically modern humans (AMH) are thought to have evolved from earlier humans, likely H. heidelbergensis, beginning around 200,000 years ago. AMH are Homo sapiens sapiens;* they are us, and they look like us, exhibiting all the usual range of physical features that are found in people today. There is some debate as to whether these early people developed fully modern behaviours (such as the full use of language, the capacity for abstract thought, and the use of symbolism to express cultural creativity) at the same time as they developed modern anatomy. However, there is little doubt that they had done so by circa 50,000 years ago. This is the period in which we can begin to rely with increased confidence on the archaeological evidence, as it becomes more plentiful from this time. Even with reasonably plentiful concrete evidence, we still cannot peer into the consciousness of these early ancestors. But we can, to a certain degree, piece together how they lived and what had significance for them. This in turn allows us some cautious extrapolation about how they may have perceived themselves and their world.

We can fairly confidently say that AMH were nomadic or semi-nomadic hunter-gatherers who moved in relatively small

---

* The reason "sapiens" is repeated twice is that there are two subspecies of Homo sapiens. One is Homo sapiens idaltu, which refers to the extinct subspecies of Homo sapiens that lived in Ethiopia between 160,000 and 154,000 years ago. The other is Homo sapiens sapiens, which refers to modern humans.

groups based on the extended family or clan. We can also be quite confident that, by about 37,000 years ago, they were doing such things as making flutes, and some scholars push the date for early musical instruments back even further. Early humans buried their dead intentionally, often with grave goods and the application of red ochre, which strongly suggests a spiritual dimension to their lives. They made art, although we don't know whether it was for self-expression, ritual, or other purposes. Magnificent examples of ancient art are found on all continents except Antarctica. Such art includes cave paintings, rock carvings, figurine sculpting, and beads. They also most probably made articles in numerous other mediums too fragile to survive the ravages of time. From this we can see that, in numerous ways, these ancient peoples were not very different from ourselves.

We cannot know how early humans perceived themselves, but again, I think we can reasonably speculate. They were tribal people who depended on the group for survival, thus rendering people and family very important. I would speculate they lived to serve and identified with the tribe more than with their individual selves. Survival of the tribe relied on both efficient food acquisition and reproduction. Though both sexes likely participated in food acquisition, only one gave birth. This would have made reproductive females central figures in the tribe, likely having a significant impact on the children's perceptions of roles and identity in the tribe. This and the prolific occurrence of female figures in early art suggests to me that, despite controversy in the early 2000s on the matter,* early humans were likely matrilineal, if indeed lineage mattered to them. Females, I believe, would also have held a prominent place in the tribe's spirituality. I believe there is sufficient evidence to support the idea that this was generally the case at least down to the Neolithic Revolution (beginning about 12,000 years ago; described later in this chapter).

---

* See Camille Paglia, *Sexual Personae* (Yale University Press, 1990) and its critical reception, described on Wikipedia; and Cynthia Eller, *The Myth of Matriarchal Prehistory* (Beacon Press, 2000).

In the late Neolithic, there came a massive change in human culture and consciousness—a change so profound and powerful that it still holds us in its grip to this day. This assertion rests on the belief that consciousness evolves over time. Furthermore, the evolution of consciousness works by similar principles to the evolution of physiology. I believe that consciousness has increased within the animal kingdom as creatures and their modes of survival have become more complex. I see the evolution of consciousness as stimulating our forebrains to develop greater capacity; increased brain capacity allowed for higher consciousness. This mutual evolution of traits over time gave us the high forehead as well as the sophisticated cultural behaviours that are signatures of anatomically modern humans. And consciousness proved to be a highly successful adaptive strategy for humankind. It was a strategy particularly well suited to the survival of our species, which lacks the speed, strength, size, teeth, or claws of competing species. We survived because of our intelligence and our abilities to communicate and cooperate, all of which are functions underpinned by consciousness.

If consciousness does indeed evolve in similar patterns to physical evolution, then it is worth taking a moment to consider the pattern of evolution. At present there appear to be two main schools of thought on this: gradualism and punctuated equilibrium. Gradualism is the concept that species evolve slowly and gradually, making relatively small, incremental changes over time. Punctuated equilibrium suggests that species remain in stasis, a relatively unchanging state, until something impels them to make sudden evolutionary shifts. In the evolution of species, I tend to favour the idea of punctuated equilibrium; however, it seems unlikely that the stasis between leaps would be a suspension of all adaptive activity. In the case of the development of culture and consciousness, I cannot help but see it as a complex blend of the two concepts. Such a state would include not only periods of stasis and sudden advancements, but also periods of slow progress. In the evolution of both the physical and the conscious aspects, the rate of change is governed by the variety of potentials within the population and the opportunities within the ecosystem it occupies.

Within any organism, mutation, as well as several other complex genetic processes, gives rise to variations. In an organism's relationship to the environment, such things as opportunity, adversity, and stability are factors that test the viability of that variation. When a variation proves to serve in coping or capitalizing on a shift in these factors, a new adaptive success has been won and the organism's "fitness" for survival is enhanced. When there is a mismatch between variation and the conditions in the ecosystem, the organism becomes less fit, less likely to survive and reproduce. I think it is the extent or intensity of the changing conditions in the environment that governs the rate of change a species undergoes. These same factors, I am sure, are the ones that have driven the evolution of human consciousness as well.

As previously stated, anatomically modern humans diverged from archaic humans approximately 200,000 years ago. These archaic humans almost certainly passed the basics of language on to H. sapiens. There is also evidence they passed on the classic hunting tools of the Stone Age: the axe and stone-tipped spear. The dialectic of culture and consciousness had already begun, and I believe it was instrumental in calling forth the appearance of our species as it is today. From what can be told from the somewhat patchy evidence, the cultural evolution of AMH proceeded fairly gradually until around 50,000 years ago, and then there may have been something of a growth spurt. It is worth noting that the only significant evolution since our full speciation is in our cultural development and, I would argue, in our consciousness.

There followed another fairly long period of gradual development that brought us to the cusp of the Neolithic Revolution. By the close of the 10th millennium BCE, there is evidence of the construction of monumental architecture by hunter-gatherers. The discovery in Turkey of the monument known as Göbekli Tepe (now a UNESCO World Heritage Site) shocked the archaeological world. It was unimaginable that hunter-gatherers could have accomplished such a feat. It is a strong statement of where these hunter-gatherers put their energy once their survival needs were met—they built beautifully decorated monolithic stone temples. The people who built Göbekli Tepe lived in a sophisticated society capable of high-level self-organization and conceptual thinking. And they, along with other tribal peoples, were now ready for a change.

The Neolithic Revolution

The adoption of agriculture by former hunter-gatherers signalled the beginning of a fundamental shift among humans. This great shift, referred to as the Neolithic Revolution, was an evolutionary leap that occurred in independent locations over a span of several thousand years. When it sprung up at the same time in two different regions, it often exhibited significant differences. The particular food resource selected for domestication depended on its availability and was likely something the local people perceived as being most useful. Change came slowly, with the roots of a movement to a sedentary way of life going back thousands of years before permanent settlements were established. This multi-dimensional matrix gives us no simple linear line of development that is easy to understand or follow. However, the trickier question is: Why did we shift toward a sedentary life of agriculture?

The main contenders for the title of the great prime motivator are as follows.

- **Climate change:** Following the last glacial event, the climate warmed and vegetation became more lush and varied. This was punctuated by a sudden cooling and drying event between 10,800 and 9500 BCE, at the very dawn of agricultural activity. It is theorized that the drier climate made annual plants (edible seeds or tubers) favoured over longer-living plants that suffered through long dry seasons. It is reasoned that the need to be on site for planting, harvesting, and storing of these crops promoted a sedentary lifestyle. These factors taken together were thought to catalyze sedentary agricultural life. Though climate change has always played a role in human evolution, modern research has suggested that its role in this case may have been sufficient to drive the Neolithic Revolution.

- **Population pressure:** Successful breeding led to population pressure, which required us to change to a more effective method of food production. However, evidence for this theory has not been well supported by modern research.

- **Social promotion:** This concept suggests that by moving to agricultural pursuits, certain industrious and opportunistic individuals could produce surplus food, which was then used to feed their less assertive neighbours and thereby gain prestige, loyalty, and allegiances. Again, evidence of social stratification is insufficient to support this model.

- **Psycho-cultural factors:** Jacques Cauvin, a French scholar and archaeologist, brought forth and popularized the radical idea that it was changes within us that drove the Neolithic. Shifts in our ability to use symbols and our evolving spirituality and imagination were seen as being of prime importance in driving the changes. This theory is basically impossible to prove empirically, as we cannot know the minds of the peoples of 12,000 years ago. However, evidence in surviving art and architecture supports the idea. Although this theory is not now seen as a prime motivator, it is seen as an important contributing element.

Thorough research and analysis has indicated that there is no single prime motivator for the momentous changes of the Neolithic. However, some factors likely played bigger roles than others. Climate and availability of local resources would have been significant. Finding a successful adaptive strategy to ensure continuance of the tribe and species in the face of such forces would have played as much a part in this shift as it had in those that preceded it.

In addition to the material forces, I believe there were less obvious subjective forces in the psyche of the peoples of the time that propelled the material changes further, faster, and more radically than could have happened otherwise. At the most basic, this unspoken call to change was a fusion of our changing relationship to the environment, the awakening of our nascent individualism and a shift in psycho-spiritual perception. Cauvin developed this idea in his concept of the Revolution of Symbols by studying the art and figurines of the Neolithic as a clue to our shifting consciousness. All these non-material elements would no doubt be propelled by the inherent human desire for growth and change, the impulse to reach beyond where we are in any given moment.

As we settled into the Neolithic Revolution, we gradually developed a radically different way of being human. Granted, we did not become a new species, but we nevertheless changed so radically in our culture and consciousness as to almost appear to have. I would argue that this was indeed a profound punctuation in our evolutionary flow, albeit a non-genetic one. It is important to keep in mind that as profound and ultimately sweeping as these changes were, they did not happen uniformly at the same time in all places. The great innovations that are the signature of this period, such as agriculture, textiles, and pottery, seem to have developed independently in various centres. Then, over time, such innovations diffused into broader hinterlands. Neolithic initiatives were dispersed over time and geography. Although these innovations affected a large percentage of the population by the beginning of the Bronze Age, it is challenging to understand the process in a modern linear manner. Relatively small regions made specific adaptations according to the available climate, resources, and any number of social factors.

The widespread adoption of agriculture was profound, beginning with a cascade of events that ultimately changed technology, the economy, and lifestyle in all but the most remote corners of the world. However, this shift did not come quickly. It is now evident that in some areas up to 19,000 years ago, humans were making considerable use of grains of various sorts in their diets. The submerged site found when the Sea of Galilee's water level dropped in 2010 contained a firmly mounted stone in one of several small huts. This stone is believed to have been dedicated to the grinding of grain. There is no indication grain was grown anywhere around the camp, making it fairly certain it was opportunistic harvesting of wild stock. However, at some point, people began to deliberately transplant or sow seed crops of a specific species. Originally, agriculture seems to have been an augmentation of a hunter-gatherer lifestyle, but gradually, for reasons unknown, production from agriculture ultimately became the dietary mainstay.

Agriculture and Its Consequences

Whatever motivated the shift from nomadic hunter-gatherer to sedentary farmer was not universally good for human beings; it came with a cost. Though it gave us civilization with its social stability, food security, and cultural specialization, it also gave us organized war, poorer nutrition, and slavery. These conditions were not widely evident among predecessors. It also initiated a ticking time bomb—overpopulation, the threat of which now looms over us.

There are two different branches of agriculture and many varieties and methods for each. Generally, people of areas that were dry or had nutrient-poor soil often found their efforts paid a better return by herding locally domesticated animals. These animals, often a prey species for earlier hunter-gatherers, were gradually domesticated to create a more dependable and safer food source. Such an economy could be nomadic, semi-nomadic, or sedentary depending on soil, climate, and animal species. This kind of an economy could be blended with farming or trading relationships with sedentary farmers. Many possibilities exist and most, I am sure, were tried.

Another innovation in domestication came with the use of domesticated animals as draft animals and later as personal transportation. This opened up a new set of possibilities for humankind's evolving civilizations. We should not overlook the role of animals in providing secondary products. Besides the obvious meat, milk, and leather, some animals provided wool or hair that could be worked into valued products. In certain regions, dung was an important fuel source, and horns could be fashioned into handy objects. For this reason, mixed farming was important, even if it was just a few prized animals associated with an otherwise vegetable-based economy.

Vegetable-based economies offered much less lifestyle variation, as they basically tied the farmer to the land. Like herders protecting their flocks from predators, farmers had to protect their crops and animals from pests and insects. Because of farming's seasonal nature, food had to be grown and stored to last through the year. As farmers must protect their crop and their harvest, they are bound to a single location. It is worth noting that we are not just talking about food production, but also specialty products, in particular, textiles. In the Near East, flax was cultivated around 8000 BCE, and charred linen has been dated to 6000 BCE at the Çatalhöyük site in what is present-day Turkey. Very early on, linen was in use in Egypt, cotton in India, and the unique process of silk production in China.

The impact of a sedentary culture that produced more food than was needed brought about profound permanent changes to the behaviour of a civilized people. The ability to acquire specialized goods, now possible with an evolving caste of full-time artisans, led to trade and wealth. Gradually societies began to stratify. The simple prestige and opportunity of an earlier shaman or chief slowly became magnified to the high dignity of a priest or king. Such transitions of society were gradual and would not be fully realized until the coming of the Bronze Age (3300 BCE to 1200 BCE).

Despite pre-agricultural societies' limited opportunities, humans' naturally opportunistic nature began to change. The temptation and availability of accumulated wealth and status enabled some to forcefully take advantage of opportunities. This behaviour could range from personal theft or murder, through raiding and all-out war. People began to build defensive structures and arm themselves, not for the hunt but for the ability to thwart fellow humans. Militarization required greater organization. Farming villages turned into walled towns, warrior castes arose, and powerful individuals commanded all who lived around them. This phenomenon awakened in the Neolithic and would not reach its full extent until the Bronze Age.

Culture and Social Order

Something subtle but profound happened at this critical turning point in human history: humankind shifted from being a part of nature to taking control. These are two distinct mindsets, and they each affect the perception of self and the world very differently. Where we had previously been subject to the order of nature, we were now beginning to impose our order on nature.

It is likely the early agricultural villages were not much more socially complex than an extended tribe of hunter-gatherers. As time passed villages became towns, and the residents had neighbours who were not directly traceable to their bloodline. Furthermore, these individuals might not share the same traditions and customs. Formerly ties of blood, custom, and need resulted in a natural cohesion. However, as the population expanded, cohesion and order would have been imposed, along with the human constructs required to support it.

Function would also impact size, form, and level of organization within a group. Tribal hunter-gatherers gain relatively little benefit from having large numbers involved with the hunt; the returns on energy spent in the hunt were balanced by the need to feed the hunters and their families. However, in an agricultural society, being able to bring a mass of people together to work leverages the dividend received for the effort. Humans by the hundreds attacking game animals is no more efficient than hunting with a band of ten—a significant waste of energy. Yet a hundred people gathering the harvest or digging an irrigation canal would potentially yield far more per unit of effort. This, of course, assumes the hundred are sufficiently cohesive and organized.

Collaboration for mutual well-being is a natural and ancient form of self-organization, yet it is easier to achieve with small groups. Organizing large groups collaboratively is a complex process that requires training in specialized systems, practices, and patience. Ancient towns would have lacked the required systems and infrastructure. Unfortunately, it is far less time-consuming to implement domination than to rely on the self-organizing principles of collaboration. With the growth of population centres, the old tribal modes began to break down. As society stratified, certain individuals gained prominence and domination over their neighbours. It seems natural that these successful people would become those to whom the masses turned for leadership. This was the beginning of a hierarchical society. As population increased and society became more complex, additional layers were added to the social pyramid.

All was well if the leader was one who could keep people in line and who contributed to the well-being of the general population. However, the question of how to maintain social order remained. There are many ways a leader might maintain authority: eliciting cooperation, coercive force, propaganda, tradition, and divine sanction, to name the most common. The last of these is particularly interesting, as it points to a social convention that was to become common in a great many cultures throughout history. We do not know when it happened, but I assume it followed the stratification of societies when the temporal and spiritual leaders of a group recognized the mutual benefit of allegiances. There would have been numerous ways such allegiances might have been structured. It appears the priest made the headman's office sacred, while the headman protected and subsidized the office of the priest. Later in this historic period, we know that some kings simply declared themselves divine and fused the roles of head of state with the head of religion. At some early point, the temporal leaders capitalized on the spiritual inclination of their people to give themselves the divine right to rule.

Religion offered another material benefit: it gave a common identity to a group of people who might be from different tribes or traditions. The common identity promoted social cohesion and inspired shared efforts in the name of the worshipped divine entities. Of course, this benefited both religious and temporal leaders significantly and paved the way for the city-states of the Bronze Age.

This era witnessed the beginnings of militarization to maintain social cohesion and obedience to authority. There is nothing like an external threat, real or imagined, to bring a people together in defence of what they have and care about. Thus, the human tendency toward territorialism and tribalism could be exploited to anchor the idea of "our land" and "our people" over larger areas and groups than was possible in earlier times. Ultimately, the idea of the superiority of "our" people, king, and gods/goddesses took root and paved the way for the invasion and conquest of other groups—the beginning of empire building. This in turn promoted a greater diversity of population, a need for social cohesion mechanisms, and a higher order of civilization. All these factors would have been brought to bear on the development of social cohesion and the submission to authority necessary for civilization's development.

Technology and Transportation
The Early Neolithic is considered pre-pottery despite its occasional use by humans in earlier times. Later in this period, pottery became more important and prolific. Initially, pottery was made by hand without the use of the potting wheel. With the invention of the potting wheel, developed in the Near East between 6000 and 4000 BCE, the growing demand from an increasing population was met.

Simple boats and barges would have been in use in this era. Yet the first vessel with a sail is dated the late 3500s BCE and calls into question whether sailboats played a significant role during this period. Though the cow and later the donkey were domesticated as draft animals, there is little evidence to suggest they were used for transportation. Rather, they were kept primarily for their meat and secondary products. Similarly, horses were initially hunted for food and it was later when they were domesticated as draft animals. By the mid-6000s BCE in the Middle East, irrigation dramatically expanded the workable farmlands.

Important changes in architecture came about with the shift to agriculture. Before this time, people were primarily nomadic and the need for shelter was restricted to simple dwellings where erection and takedown did not require a large investment of energy. As people settled near their crops, more permanent dwellings became practical. In the Fertile Crescent, mud bricks replaced the brush-and-hide shelters and were originally built in a circular or oval configuration common to the region. The early villages and towns followed this design. However, with the shift toward dependence on agriculture, the building style changed to the rectilinear format, and structures were more densely packed together for efficiency. This change in design might be indicative of a general transformation in mindset of the time. It represented a shift from an organic and fluid lifestyle to a more rigid and efficient model. With this shift came the proto-cities Jericho and Çatalhöyük, and ultimately the founding of Uruk, the first true city.

Spirituality
On the northern edge of the Fertile Crescent in about 9500 BCE, a group of hunter-gatherers built Göbekli Tepe, which is considered to be one of the oldest religious monuments known today. The stonework was exquisite, with not just one circular temple but twenty on the site. And this vast amount of fine stonework was done with only stone tools, as they had nothing else. These were a nomadic or semi-nomadic people with no evidence of permanent habitation around the site. But there is ample evidence of large gatherings, judging from the volume of animal bones found at the site. There must have been a lot of people working on such a monumental task, and those people would need to have been fed by surplus food from others. This was a

rich hunter-gatherer society, and it must have been relatively populous to support the economy of scale required for such a venture. And this was no flash-in-the-pan endeavour; the site was occupied with added works over centuries. Interpreting the meaning and intentions of ancient cultures through the lens of the modern mind is an uncertain task. However, I think one profound conclusion can be drawn: When there were enough people with sufficient surplus resources, they turned their capacity toward spiritual expression. In this, the monument builders of the following centuries were not alone.

By 5000 BCE, with the emergence of the Atlantic Neolithic period, many sites begin to show up on the Atlantic coastal areas. In the latter part of this period, sites developed along the Mediterranean coastline, as well as one notable site in the south of what is now Egypt.

A similar archaeological phenomenon to Göbekli Tepe was found submerged off the coast of Israel and dated around 3300 BCE, though the situation by this time is quite different. People were building permanent residential structures that would have taken notable time, energy, and resources away from the construction of sacred structures. However, in addition to the residences, the site had a semi-circular arrangement of six decorated megaliths arcing around a spring, each weighing at least 590 kilograms. This strongly suggests a sacred monument with a ritual purpose.

The building of monumental structures and complexes continued throughout the Neolithic and into the Bronze Age. It would dwindle toward the middle of 2000 BCE and ended conclusively around 1200 BCE. In that vast expanse of time, a wide variety of sacred sites developed. These included grave structures, stone circles, processional ways, temples, and various earthworks. Apart from earthworks intended for defence, the structures would have served symbolic ritual functions, and they raise questions about the societies that built them. Even the great stone circles, often considered as a celestial calendar device, could have been important for ritual purposes. No farmer plants or harvests exclusively according to rigid calendar dates, given seasonal fluctuations in the weather. However, I believe the ability to predict solstices and equinoxes would have had significant mystical power and importance.

From the pre-dawn of civilization through the many innovations of the Neolithic and into the Bronze Age, when human beings had the wealth, resources, and organization, they pursued spiritual understanding. They made conscious attempts to understand and develop a relationship with the mysteries of life and the cosmos. The collapse of the Bronze Age civilizations may have brought the megalithic era to a close, but it was merely a hiatus in the material record of our spiritual endeavours. As soon as the next wave of civilization took hold, we resumed building sacred structures and have continued doing so to this day. Spirituality is central to what we have been and what we remain.

Other artifacts also bear testimony to the human proclivity toward spirituality. Art in a variety of forms and materials can be found throughout the Neolithic and, in fact, some date back well into the Upper Paleolithic. Early in the Neolithic, jewellery was likely worn for either aesthetic pleasure or magical protection. There is a widespread consensus among scholars that early cultures were not socially stratified and therefore would not use jewellery as a status symbol. Stone carving on megalithic elements was almost undoubtedly related to the spiritual purposes of the megalith itself. Pottery, when it came into common use, was generally decorated, and in the later Neolithic, it was glazed. Glazing has the practical advantage of making earthenware water-tight, yet some glazing and other decoration on vessels is mysterious. Cultures generally had signature styles of decorating pottery that must have meant something to them.

There is also the matter of the relatively abundant finds of figurines, and the controversies they have engendered. Essentially, the figurines from prehistory come in three main motifs: animal, anthropomorphic, and human. This makes sense in that they represent the ancients' two most dynamic and important life forms along with a third imaginary conflation of themselves. Art venerating animals seems natural for societies that relied heavily on animals for food and by-products. Whether the figurines were totems, charms, or just objects of veneration, they would almost certainly be of mystical significance. Anthropomorphic figures are no doubt related, somehow blending the attributes of the spirit of humans with that of animals. This is a very ancient art form that predates the Neolithic and was practised into the Bronze Age. Given the nature of hunter-gatherer existence, these figures do not seem surprising at all.

What is remarkable about the human figures is that the vast majority are of sexually mature females, with the secondary sexual characteristics exaggerated, particularly the breasts and hips/buttocks. Such figures are also of great antiquity, predating the rise of the Neolithic by as much as 30,000 years. This has given rise to theories of goddess cults, fertility cults, and matriarchal cultures. These suggestions were met with strong negative reaction in some scholarly circles. There is no clear indication of matriarchal societies in the cultural remains from the late Paleolithic or Neolithic periods. However, as human societies developed, there is evidence that they were in some instances female-led, and some tribal cultures continue to use matriliny to this day as a method of reckoning descent. Overall, the egalitarian nature of ancient cultures from that period indicates that they were not hierarchical, making strong traditions of leadership exclusively by either sex unlikely. None of this does anything to explain the profusion of the "Venus" and "goddess" figurines that were typical of the period.

Because of the mystique and great importance of human fertility in the Paleolithic and Early Neolithic, I cannot imagine that fertility cults would not have been extant. Given that needed resources originally came from Earth and Earth's offspring (the fruits and animals essential to life), I think it would have been inevitable for early humans to experience Earth as the Great Mother. This is an old archetype, and it persists in our thoughts and language to this day.

Jacques Cauvin put forward the idea that Neolithic female figures were indeed goddess symbols, and that the images of male animals, especially the bull, were introduced as the male counterpart. It seems likely to me that we may have entered the Neolithic with our chief anthropomorphic deity as a goddess. It was long after the domestication of animals that the essence of the masculine would begin to be felt. Herding would have brought us into consistent contact with the fact that without a ram there is no lamb. Further, the male not only began life but stamped its offspring with its characteristics. Agriculture would have impressed upon us a similar idea; earth is not fertile without water from the sky and the mountains, which are archetypally associated with the masculine. This shift in thought would have profound implications as societies began to stratify, and eventually militarize, setting the stage for the startling shifts to come in the Bronze Age. While this conception of the masculinization of early societies is conjecture, it does seem to be borne out by characteristics of the Proto-Indo-European peoples who would become the rootstock of Western civilization.

Transition to the Bronze Age

The Neolithic Revolution began the ending of a way of life that humanity had followed for the entirety of our previous existence. It changed what it was to be human and ushered in waves of further change, not only to our cultures but also to the ways in which we think. It was catalyzed by an interplay of both external and internal motivators, interactions that were expressed in slightly different ways in different times and places. Culture, both material and spiritual, changed slowly at first, then with gathering speed. Toward the end of this period, relatively large culturally homogeneous populations formed and developed unique styles and traditions. Around the same time, the smelting of copper began to make limited amounts of this wonderful substance available, but its malleability generally limited its uses to jewellery and symbolic weaponry. At this point, we were standing on the threshold of the ending of the Stone Age and the dawn of the Bronze Age, and a whole new wave of technical, social, and spiritual innovations.

As metals go, unalloyed copper is quite soft, ductile, and not able to hold an edge well, which limits its use. However, it does not take a lot of the right kind of substance added to copper to change those properties significantly and produce a far more useful product. One of the minerals that produces this result is arsenic. The first implements containing this alloy were made in the 5th millennium BCE, on the Iranian Plateau. Because of the frequent occurrence of arsenic in copper ores, and the naturally high concentrations of arsenic in the ores of the region, it is thought that the first incidences of the making of arsenical bronze were lucky accidents. However, the advantages of the new alloy would have been quickly noticed, and inquisitive people would have sought to understand what was going on. It appears they eventually understood the process and began deliberately adding arsenic to create the alloy.

As the technology began to spread, an unknown smelter of metals made another great innovation to the process. The addition of tin to copper makes a far more useful metal, the qualities of which are quite similar to arsenical bronze. The advantage of tin bronze was not an improved alloy but an improved process and end product. Tin bronze was superior to arsenical bronze in that the alloying process could be more easily controlled and the resulting alloy was easier to cast. Unlike arsenic, tin is not toxic, making both mining and smelting operations safer. Tin bronze artifacts have been discovered as early as the mid-4th millennium BCE, but did not come into broad use and distribution until the 3rd millennium BCE. Even with its early start, it would be many centuries before western Eurasia would have general access to bronze. Nevertheless, tin bronze was a key innovation that, along with others, would significantly change the world and the people in it.

With the advent of the Bronze Age came the first undisputed use of written language. It evolved in Mesopotamia, apparently as an outgrowth of much earlier primitive systems for the accounting of goods. Continued growth of population and the increasing societal complexity pushed the early systems through several developmental iterations until around 2700 BCE, when Mesopotamian cuneiform appeared as a versatile full-fledged written language. Like other useful human innovations, the skill spread within the region and beyond. With this development came the first fragments of recorded history. Limited in scope and no doubt with significant bias, they nevertheless require a lot less interpretation to grasp than buried artifacts.

The Proto-Indo-European Migration

Everything changed with the coming of written history. We now get a far better idea of who people were and what they were doing. However, there is one more critical event in the early Bronze Age that preceded recorded history and effectively changed Western history forever. The Proto-Indo-European peoples, as they are now known, arose on the Pontic Steppes of Eastern Europe, and were the offspring of a long history of human settlement in that area. They were remarkable for several reasons. They domesticated the horse and certainly had very early use of the wheel. Further, it seems they set the tone for Western civilization from their era to the present.

It was debated for a long time whether these mysterious people originated on the Pontic Steppes or in Anatolia. Recent studies synthesizing linguistics, archaeology, and genetic information have pointed undeniably to the Pontic Steppes. Scholars have also been able to reasonably date and map the movement of these ambitious people from their homeland on the Steppes into much of the rest of Western Eurasia. The scope of this immigration was amazing.

It seems likely that migrations out of the Steppes were initiated by something called the 5.9 kiloyear event. It was one of the most intense aridification events during the Holocene Epoch. It occurred around 3900 BCE, 5900 years BP (before present), ending a wet period that started in the late 8th millennium BCE. The 5.9 kiloyear event is thought to have upset population distribution over the known world, driving people toward the great river valleys as water sources and farmlands dried out. The Steppes would have become colder and much drier, putting the pinch on the mixed-agricultural economies of the region. In response, people likely moved either into the valleys or toward a more nomadic herding economy. Or they left the dry plains altogether to "seek greener pastures." With the domestication of the horse around this time, those on the Steppes would have had a significant advantage over other cultures in developing a herding culture or emigrating, or both. It appears that around 3900 BCE, a significant proportion of the population left and began to enter new and already occupied lands.

The nature of the emigrations from the Steppes is not completely clear. Scholars such as Marija Gimbutas have suggested waves of mounted warriors poured off the Steppes and took the lands of Old Europe by bloody conquest. This theory as a sole cause for the collapse of the Danube cultures has now fallen into disrepute. However, it does appear that the early Indo-Europeans were warlike and had the advantage of being the world's first mounted warriors. They were a heroic masculinist culture, judging from the cultures that arose from the lands they invaded or influenced.

Yet military prowess was not the only way to penetrate, influence, and eventually dominate another culture. There was also acculturation and assimilation. I think the two most likely methods would have been trade and what I call "passive invasion." The Proto-Indo-Europeans had both something to trade, namely bronze, and a way to effectively transport it, the horse. If they were emigrating from their homeland with no preconceived destination, this would make them ideal candidates as traders. They could easily impress the locals with their goods, horses, style of weapons, self-decoration, and deportment. Even if they did not settle in an area, they would gradually inoculate it with their culture, and to some extent, their language.

Passive invasion is a scenario where a headman, his group, and their livestock enter a new area and insinuate themselves upon land not actively farmed for crops. Livestock can be quite successfully raised on lands with poor soil or in a location that is too dry for crops. The locals may not have appreciated their new neighbours, yet the armed and aggressive presence probably made the Proto-Indo-Europeans intimidating. There may have been occasional skirmishes and there almost certainly would have been social tensions, yet there are indications the Proto-Indo-European groups had techniques to manage discontent. There is evidence to suggest that a typical tactic for smoothing the waters and ultimately gaining allies lay in feasting them. If the invading group had sufficient livestock to support feasts with generous servings of meat, and probably beer, the locals might be won over or at least left with some feelings of indebtedness. The headman of the new group would gain considerable prestige, and the indebtedness of the locals might have led to him becoming a big man in the district.

I imagine the three methods—warfare, trading, and passive invasion—would have been used at various times and places during the Proto-Indo-European migrations. But even so, how is it that they became so very successful at dominating the cultures they encountered? The factors already mentioned would have served them, but I think there was another invisible factor. It seems to me that an impetus to change was brewing up in the collective psyche. Cultures of the time were starting to stratify more and more; the goddess and fertility cults were losing their power to hold the hearts of the people. I think the transition from hunting and gathering to agriculture provided reasons for this latter swing of allegiances. The concept of masculine gods of the sky and mountains that provided the water to nourish the crops would become more comprehensible and desirable.

The lure of accumulated wealth, power, and prestige would have also fired the imagination. This might have been intoxicating for men seeing successful modelling of a male-dominated, masculine-centred culture. It well might have fired up the natural dominant attribute that supported men to win a mate and then defend her. Similarly, the inherent willingness to defend could fairly easily be co-opted toward a more aggressive militaristic approach. With accumulated wealth, a society had the means to defend their own or steal from others. I believe the social models demonstrated by the Proto-Indo-Europeans were appealing and had repurposed ancient instinctual inclinations in people unconsciously restless for change. This, then, was the creative power that gave the Proto-Indo-European peoples such lasting impact. It was not that their numbers imposed change, but rather that their societal model catalyzed change that wanted to happen.

Population increases, improved farming techniques and greater social organization pushed civilization forward, deepening the changes that the Neolithic Revolution had begun. Towns became cities, and then cities became city-states and kingdoms. With this growth came increased specialization and social stratification, which ultimately led to the steep social pyramid topped by the king and supported by the masses of the under-classes. Increased militarism saw the development of well-organized and -outfitted armies, capable of defending a walled city or attacking one. The use of the horse, particularly to pull war chariots, added to the mobility and striking force. Laws and religions began to be codified, solidifying social norms and cementing cultural identity. Much of the trappings of what we would call civilization were formed in this period, shaping the way we live to this day.

Cultures and Consciousness

We have had a look at our origins from bipedalism to anatomical modernity and through to the foundations of civilization. While tracing this story gives us a good working idea of our evolutionary path, it does not define what makes us essentially human. The defining factors must be things we have been doing for at least as long as we have been anatomically modern, that have occurred across geographical space and relatively consistently throughout time, and that continue in some form as widespread practices to this day. I have developed an unordered list of what I think are the main elements that define what is essentially human.

Overarching characteristics
- **Intelligent:** capable of abstract thought and planning
- **Verbal:** command of a complex language
- **Social:** gregarious and collaborative
- **Adaptable:** capable of adapting to virtually any environment on Earth
- **Protective:** ready to defend child, mate, tribe, or territory

Behaviours validated by archaeology
- **Hunting and gathering:** collecting, extracting, and harvesting a wide range of foods and medicines
- **Food preparation:** processing, cooking, and preserving foods
- **Manufacture:** tools, pigments, jewellery, pottery, metallurgy
- **Art and self-adornment:** painting, rock art, sculpture, jewellery, costume, tattoo, body modification
- **Spiritual expressions:** figurines, grave goods, monument building, ritual
- **Music:** creating and using musical instruments
- **Trading:** exchanging goods through barter and/or currency exchange

Implied behaviours not clearly validated by archaeology
- **Elaborate education of our young:** inevitable for our evolution
- **Mythmaking/etiology:** assumed from evidence of spiritual expressions
- **Singing and dancing:** assumed from the use of musical instruments
- **Use of entheogens and intoxicants:** assumed from the prevalence in nearly all recorded cultures and with some archaeological inference

Although we humans lacked the size, speed, or natural weapons of other creatures, we have obviously demonstrated our capacity to thrive and survive. This capacity is derived from our essential characteristics: our intelligence, ability to communicate, and proclivity for collaboration. These characteristics gave rise to the ability to problem solve at the group level, thereby significantly leveraging our strength and intelligence. Our group problem solving is further supported by our protectiveness of what is important to us and, somewhat paradoxically, by our willingness to grow, change, and move. This is what gave us the evolutionary edge.

These basic characteristics, in dynamic interaction with our needs and the environment, brought forth adaptive behaviours that nourished and supported us and our evolution. Not just the obvious necessities of tool making, planning the hunt, or teaching our children survival skills, but also pushing us to learn to sing, dance, and make music in order to form social bonds and develop shared joy. Other behaviours, such as developing art, myth, and spiritual ritual, offered outlets for some of the higher expressions of our humanity: aesthetics, identity, and spirituality. Such expressions offer a different order of nourishment than food and safety, but they invariably arise once physical well-being is achieved and therefore appear to be only slightly less necessary to health and wholeness. We are creatures that still need to call on these common characteristics and behaviours, to varying degrees, regardless of how we may dress them up in modern times.

Our species has been so effective as to have brought ourselves to the cusp of our undoing. In the future, a large part of what will allow us to become a sustainable world community lies in our ability to understand our essential natures and behaviours. With that knowledge, the task is then to balance the satisfaction of our needs with the available resources in our environment in a sustainable manner. The reshaping and redirecting of our essence will set the path of our future evolutionary success.

An Ambiguous Legacy

The events spanning the Neolithic Revolution through to the dawn of recorded history in the Bronze Age saw the rise and development of civilization and what it meant to be a human being. In this epochal shift we stopped being nomadic, developed from modest tribes to concentrated populations of many thousands, witnessed religious transformation, saw tribal customs and taboos replaced by sweeping social law and custom, changed our diets, our roles, our technologies, our self-image.

Good nutrition, hygiene, medical science, wealth, social order, and infrastructure have made life better for most of us, certainly in the West. However, not all the outcomes of civilization have been beneficial gifts. Civilization, like so many things, also has its dark underbelly, and we are starting to see it.

Our archaic instinctual natures and vestigial survival strategies plague us when they play out in the civilized context where they are distorted and exaggerated. This is not because civilization is evil or corrupt; it is rather that the changes that civilizations wrought have not yet caught up to our unconscious drivers. Similarly, with our drives and strategies, we are not corrupt or evil. There was no "fall" from a "golden age of humankind." We did not fall anywhere; we evolved. We were not somehow sundered from the divine; we reconceived our relationship to it. It is the unique interactions of the archaic mind with the modern situation that makes for problems.

It is important to bear in mind that we were anatomically modern humans for at least 100,000 years before the Neolithic, and we were behaviourally modern for approximately the last 40,000 years of that period. For a very long time, we developed patterns of behaviour and modes of thought that were suited to specks of population dispersed in a vast, wild environment. This deeply embedded the fundamental drives and strategies that I refer to. In that environment, they had natural checks and balances. Then, in a few thousand years, we revised the environment to an amazing degree and developed a whole new way of being. And that changed everything.

For example, a healthy degree of opportunism was important to a hunter-gatherer. They had to be able to recognize and seize resources where and when they found them. The exigencies of living in a time and region tested by glacial maximums or desertification would have made this especially important. Countering this opportunism would have been the fact that resources were often rare, hard to store, and another burden to carry when the tribe moved, so greed and hoarding were not practical. Also, in the social context of the tribe, greed and hoarding were dangerously unacceptable. Similarly, the tendency to dominance and aggression might help secure a mate or defend a kill from other predators, but it would have had to be carefully modulated in the tribal context for the sake of all. In the modern context, these same tendencies could be escalated and exalted to the point where they could, did, and do underpin war, exploitation, and slavery. It is the changed context and the unchanged drives and strategies that create the problems.

Perhaps one of the most obvious and poignant examples of an adaptive strategy becoming maladaptive can be seen in our dietary habits. For millennia, we ate pretty much everything we could find, and rightly so, given the scarcity and uncertainty of food resources. In times of plenty, it was adaptive to feast, gorging on the recent kill or find, because next week could be lean. However, in our affluent resource-rich situation, starvation is not the threat—obesity, diabetes, and heart disease are. We simply have not gotten over the impulse to eat when food is there, and this impulse is killing many of us before our time. This is a case of maintaining strategies that at one time were adaptive and had natural checks and balances, but are now often unchecked and have shifted from adaptive to destructive.

The issue is not that humans are inherently flawed or that civilization is inevitably corrupt; the issue is a failure to adapt to the way we have changed our world. It is a failure of consciousness, self-awareness, and choice. And it is something we must address for the sake of our continued survival.

Chapter Four

Evolution of Western Culture

Looking at recorded history with an eye to seeing how the essential nature of human beings continued to evolve and unfold under the influence of civilization provides information about the worldviews of the cultures that gave rise to the modern West. Ultimately, this book seeks answers that will support us to move forward successfully in the face of the coming challenging times.

- What is it that remains essentially human after thousands of years of civilization?
- What of that human essence will impede us and what will support us in moving forward?
- What traits have been amplified or acquired through civilization?
- Which of those traits will impede us and which will support us in moving forward?

The bias toward Western culture is not because of any inherent superiority of that culture, but because the ideas, ethos, and intentions of Western culture have permeated much of the modern world, and many see the Western way as the path to a desirable lifestyle. Thus it is worth examining the themes, forces, and patterns that have revealed themselves as our cultures have developed and become more complex; how those patterns impact us now; and potentially how they will impact us into the future.

Western culture did not evolve in a vacuum. Trade with non-Europeans dates back into late prehistory in Europe, and with the trade of goods came also exchanges of religion, philosophy, and technology. Major wars of conquest date back into the middle of the 1st millennium BCE; in particular, the back-and-forth struggle of the Greek and Persian empires created penetrations of culture both ways, including non-material exchanges. So, the West has long been influenced by the East and vice versa. Nevertheless, Europe and Asia formed distinct cultures, with distinct ways of seeing the world, although, with globalization and world markets, the Western vision seems to be overtaking or at least influencing traditional cultures around the world.

THE WESTERN WORLDVIEW

Reality is a slippery thing; not only has the nature of reality been endlessly debated, but its very existence has been doubted. However, I believe that our way of perceiving reality profoundly affects our daily life whether we are particularly conscious of it or not. Understanding this is especially important to those of us who would approach life consciously, as perception is the very foundation of our existence. To quote a wise man, Moshe Feldenkrais: "If you know what you're doing, you can do what you want."

I believe there is some form of consistent reality that lies beyond our human limitations to perceive fully. This idea is supported by science through observation and measurement, though some challenge the philosophical basis for the science. However, a critical caveat comes with this belief—an external reality cannot be considered objectively in any meaningful way. The reason is that every human gains sensory, intuitive, and imaginative impressions of the external reality and then interprets it according to their personal internal set of filters and experiences. Therefore, humans cannot reasonably claim to be able to describe an objective reality despite the paradoxical likelihood that there is one; we simply cannot know that reality without adulterating it with our perception.

For the moment, let us accept that the reality we experience is subjective. If that is the case, how is it that we ever agree or get anything done? The key lies in mutuality, especially in what the philosophers call "universals." These universals are such things as colours, shapes, textures, temperatures, and any characteristic that can be deemed to be the same, or in most instances, workably similar. We can develop a mutual reality based on agreement on the definition of each universal. In this way, the world becomes workable; we can communicate, plan, and achieve things because we have agreed to a host of definitions.

Reality comes down to energy structured by consciousness to yield a manifestation that is perceived, interpreted, and formulated into an organized system within the mind of the individual. To make it workable, an expansive set of agreed-upon definitions are taught to our young, so that each individual can then participate in the collective world and its events. Each reproductive couple that brings forth another human life perpetuates these agreements by teaching them to their child, and thus the definitions continue into the future.

From this understanding, we can surmise a number of things about the human experience. The first is that there is uniqueness to each individual's subjective experience of an external reality. Second, that the individual's reality is shaped from their perceptions of that external reality, and that those perceptions are in turn interpreted through the individual's unique psychic processes. Because these psychic processes are so pervasive, powerful, and generally unconscious, interpretation significantly influences the ability to perceive, therefore blurring the distinction between perception and interpretation. Each of us, as well as our overall culture, has a need to organize perceptions and interpretations in some sort of cogent, ordered system. This becomes the worldview of the individual and/or culture, which can range from fully mystical and magical to the starkly reductionist scientific perspective.

As Gary B. Palmer puts it in his 1996 book *Toward a Theory of Cultural Linguistics*, a worldview can be described as "the fundamental cognitive orientation of a society, a subgroup, or even an individual. It encompasses natural philosophy, fundamental existential and normative postulates or themes, values (often conflicting), emotions, and ethics ..." (pp. 113–14). Simply put, it is how we see our world and everything in and about it. A very important characteristic of a worldview is that it is so ubiquitous that we are generally unaware it is affecting every perception, interpretation, interaction, and decision that we make; it is the water, and we are the fish.

Regardless of whether one holds a conventional Western worldview or a variant of it, or a very different worldview altogether, we all have a worldview. And a worldview, like the egoic personality, is necessary to navigate life and function effectively in the world. A worldview also affects our ability to perceive and interpret the world, skewing our impressions to conform to our already-held worldview. Thus, a worldview is both essential, yet potentially detrimental, to our growth and understanding.

PREHISTORY

To understand the roots of the Western worldview, how it developed, and its impact on our present situation and future evolution, we need to incorporate what we know of the essence of humanity from prehistory and use our imagination to layer onto those essences the forces of ever more complex societies that followed in recorded times. All those societies, and our ideas about them, have influenced the Western worldview.

I suspect the worldview of Paleolithic people would have been significantly different from ours, their sense of identity deeply embedded in nature and the tribe. The idea that they were an intimate part of the ecology would likely be so self-evident to them that it would not warrant much, if any, thought. Life would have been immediate and rather simple; there would not be much concern about one's long-range plans or career and no way to acquire much material wealth. Life would be about survival: reproduction, gaining the food and materials necessary for life, and protecting life from predation. As groups were small family and tribal units, I imagine people who were quite social, caring, and collaborative.

In a society lacking the ability to accumulate and store wealth, there would have been little to gain and much to lose if competition weakened the group's social and practical bonds. The exception would likely have been for mating purposes; this would have created an intergroup issue, given the necessity to avoid inbreeding. Because tribalism and territorialism would have been adaptive strategies in most circumstances in that era, it is likely most people would exhibit those traits to varying degrees. That being the case, I imagine intergroup relations to have been somewhat formal and to have followed ritual and taboo to prevent conflicts that neither group would risk. Intergroup marriage and perhaps trade or gift giving would also smooth the social patterns. Nonetheless, I imagine most individuals would be more at ease in their own small tribal unit. In all, I believe, nature gave these people enough challenges without bickering and competing among themselves on any level. Life could sometimes be harsh, but in times of safety and plenty, I am sure people then did what most of us do now—kick back and have a good time.

I imagine a cheerful, hearty people, keenly present in the moment and usually at relative peace with themselves and their world. This is not to idealize the people of this era, but to highlight the simplicity and continuity that a hunter-gatherer culture would likely know. Despite its hardships and challenges, this simple survival-focused way of life and the worldview that perpetuated it was successful for a very long time, allowing our species to gradually mature until the next great leap forward.

As our species gradually entered the Neolithic, we would initially have carried the same mindset as in the Paleolithic. But as the social, economic, and technological scene changed, so would our worldview. The ability to acquire wealth and property would propel us to be more defensive and aggressive to protect these things. Even the herders who remained nomadic would have had to protect their prized herds from both men and beasts. The separation from nature, the acquisition of wealth, greater opportunities, and aggression would have allowed the more dominant of a group's members to move into special status in the community. Very slowly the tribe, now living in villages, would begin to stratify, giving rise to the concept of one's station within the group. Eventually this stratification would take place in both the secular and spiritual sectors, while technological advances would eventually lead to specialized trades or professions. Within their village, people would know the big man and high priest or priestess; they would slowly become acquainted with social roles and dominance in a way they never had before. Our worldview of who we were and how we related to others had begun to slowly and markedly shift.

I think it is safe to assume the transition from hunting/gathering to farming/herding was a gradual and lengthy process, and not a shock to the psyches of those involved. Settlements probably began with established extended family groups. With the addition of other local groups to the village, they would no doubt be accepted as a similar people from a different family. Stratification of society would have similarly come slowly and therefore place relatively little stress on roles and the self-identity of the individuals. Overall, I imagine a gregarious people within their village, yet with a cautious and suspicious outlook on others not of their group. The stressors of civilization would not have had that much effect, and life would be fairly simple, though certainly not carefree—survival, regardless of the economy, remained a serious business.

The discovery of metal smelting, like that of agriculture, dispersed slowly from a few localized areas and initially did not have a large cultural impact. With the discovery of bronze metallurgy, things began to shift. Tools and weapons improved and exacerbated the changes already underway. Other advances in the technologies of farming and irrigation, potting, textiles, and domestication came along. In the latter category, the domestication of the horse would ultimately lead to efficient wheeled vehicles, which had a profound effect in the Bronze Age. All this allowed for greater diversity and specialization in livelihoods and forms of goods and, thereby, wealth. Hierarchies grew with the social changes, giving human beings a clear knowledge of their identity and place in the social context. Wealth, status, and prestige would have become important factors in a shifting concept of self-identity and belonging, particularly in the higher classes.

With larger towns and proto-cities eventually evolving into cities, there was an ever-increasing demand for mechanisms to support social cohesion and order. One such mechanism for creating social cohesion was religion, which utilized the natural inclination toward spirituality and directed it into a unifying consistent form. Another mechanism was the great leader who commanded troops that ensured his will was done. The spread of the culture and ideologies of the Proto-Indo-Europeans had a significant effect on the development of order in society. Our identity and relationships shifted; the West became masculinist with the heroic male leader at the top of the hierarchy, supported by a structured system of warriors beneath him and blessed by a male-dominated pantheon of gods and their priests. This shift separated members of society not only by wealth, power, and profession, but also by gender.

The concept of general conquest came into being as the traits of militancy, city-state or regional identity, and a cultivated sense of superiority combined with greater opportunities for wealth and power. Wars of subjugation became a lucrative, if dangerous, proposition. Rather than raiding a neighbouring village for a few sheep or goods, a king could muster his army to take a region and retain control of it for his continued benefit. The age of empires had begun, and the thirst for conquest and expansion seemed insatiable.

On the cusp of the historic period, people would feel the pressures of civilization quite strongly. They would face threats of attack from other would-be nations, and the presence of strangers, slaves from their conquests, traders, and immigrants. As cities offer a higher degree of anonymity than villages and therefore increase the likelihood of mischief and crime, the gains had to be guarded against opportunism. Kings, backed by their religious counterparts, could now rule with an iron fist. Conscription into the military, forced labour, and heavy taxes would add pressures to life, to say nothing of wars and famines. Self-identity might be locked by birth, with little hope of professional or social advancement; if your father was a tanner, it was likely you would follow in his trade. Marriage and sexuality might be governed by the state religion and so on. In short, people of this era would suffer the pressures and limitations that echo down to this day: the era of neurosis—with its symptoms of stress (depression, anxiety, etc.)—had begun.

These were a people who had been gradually forced into conformity, cohesion, and compliance by the needs of their society, essentially trading their freedom and independence for the relative safety and opportunities of life in a permanent and organized centre of population. Given the pressures of this kind of life, I believe such people would be generally fearful and suspicious of those outside their immediate circle. They would likely focus on their best interests by conforming to societal requirements to avoid trouble, yet take advantage of the situation when it appeared safe. Separation from nature would be common among urban dwellers, with the human-built environment perceived as safer than rural areas. Generally, I would see people in the urban Bronze Age as similar to our modern selves, only perhaps suffering from even higher levels of stress due to the lack of safety, hygiene, and medicine along with the immediate possibility of war, famine, or plague.

By the end of the Bronze Age, we had developed much of the worldview that persists into modern times: masculinism, the right of might, moralism, the right to exploit resources both human and natural, a fiercely defended sense of group identity, and imperialism. As survival became more certain, at least in the upper classes, dominance, wealth, power, and prestige became larger factors, as did the switch from the emphasis on the clan to the aggrandizement of the individual. To this end, our instincts were indulged or exploited to varying degrees. One could betray a friend for wealth or buy a slave who was no more to you than livestock—opportunities that encouraged depersonalization and separation. And while you lived, you could be blessed or damned by divine forces you could not even see but were obliged to believe in. We were becoming a notably different creature than we had been—the civilized human.

The advent of science was inspired by the philosophers of Classical Greece, who introduced the idea that nature could be explained through reason and structure rather than mythology and magic. However, people had been making useful compounds and extracts for a long time, culminating in the capacity to smelt metals. This ability must have impressed upon people their own prowess in shaping nature; they were developing the god-like capacity to change the nature of things. It was most apparent in the art of smelting, where sacred essence could be drawn from stones to create the treasured metals. This process would have cemented in the minds of people the idea that not only could they compound, alter, and extract things from nature, but they could actually effect a transmutation of something natural into something not found in nature. This was a profound leap, and one that would play a major role in the ultimate evolution of our species.

HISTORY

Numerous cultures have had rich traditions of oral history; however, the formal history of a people begins when they possess the capacity to write and begin to keep records. Writing, like various other human inventions, evolved in different places and progressed over time. The early development of writing took place in the Bronze Age, probably driven by the increasing complexity of developing cultures and economies. By the 2nd millennium BCE, literacy existed in various parts of the Eastern Mediterranean, notably in the Egyptian, Minoan, Mycenaean, and Canaanite cultures. Then a terrible disruption occurred in these regions and the Bronze Age collapsed. Theories abound as to the cause, but multiple major powers across the Mediterranean and Near East were suddenly extinguished. At this time, we could say that history in the West sputtered.

Literacy in the Greek world seems to have been interrupted through the cultural fragmentation of the Greek Dark Ages (1100 to 900 BCE). However, by the mid to late 8th century BCE, a new Greek alphabet was adapted from the Phoenician alphabet, which the Greeks modified to create the first truly alphabetic writing system. This alphabetic system was broadly adopted throughout much of the Mediterranean region and would eventually branch and be adopted by other language groups in lands far beyond.

The 8th century BCE marks the beginning of what is known as the Archaic period in Greece. It also marks what the German philosopher Karl Jaspers called the Axial Age. According to Jaspers, between the 8th and the 3rd centuries BCE, there was an unprecedented upwelling of human intellectual activity that has shaped human thought to this day. This activity took place in the primary centres of civilization of the time: China, India, Middle East, and Greece. According to Jaspers, this activity, though concurrent, took place without cross-cultural fertilization and gave rise to unique regional expressions. While many scholars have accepted Jaspers's concept as a key historical component of thought and religion, in recent times the theory has been attacked for various reasons. Regardless, when considering the facts, it cannot be denied that there was an amazing proliferation of previously unknown thought throughout this period. Something was happening. In China there was Confucius and Lao-Tse, India produced the Upanishads and the Buddha, Persia brought forth Zarathustra, and from Palestine there emerged a string of biblical prophets. In Greece, the entire school of pre-Socratic thought came into being through the poets Homer, Hesiod, and others. Call it what you will, it was an era of profound human advancement.

In Greece the Archaic period showed a strong revival of culture and economy, and a surge of colonization on the coastlines of the Mediterranean and Black Sea. The population began to reorganize into what would become the classic city-state, the polis. Permanent temples of significant size were built. But perhaps the most important aspect was the increase in intellectual activity. Thales of Miletus (624–546 BCE) was considered by many, including Aristotle, to be the first true philosopher. Thales used reason and empirical observation to arrive at his concepts rather than relying on mythical explanations of how the world worked, which was a profound shift in Western thought. Thales was considered to be one of the first scientists, and his approach gave rise to a lineage of philosophers who followed his methods of reason and deduction. In short, Thales gave birth to Western philosophy and the ethos that underpins science.

Most literature in the Archaic period was poetry; the poets Hesiod and especially Homer gave rise to a strong poetic tradition. It is also believed that Thespis (circa 600 BCE) initiated the tradition of the tragedies and may have been the first to appear on stage as a character in a play. The tradition of life-sized freestanding human stone sculptures began in this period, and pottery decoration shifted from geometric patterns to figurative scenes. Coinage was struck for the first time in Greece in the 6th century BCE and was quickly adopted over a wide area. Over the approximately three centuries of the Archaic period, Greece reinvented itself and set the stage for the Classical period.

The intellectual and cultural momentum of the Archaic period built to a crescendo in the Classical period, generally considered to span 510 to 323 BCE. Much of the foundations of politics, architecture, sculpture, scientific thought, theatre, literature, and philosophy of Western civilization is derived from this period. The Romans, heavily influenced by the Greeks, cemented this cultural legacy and later carried the Greek ideals and ideas across the breadth of the Roman Empire.

Interestingly, this extremely fecund period was not one of peace and tranquility. Early in the period, the Persians attacked Greece in response to the Ionian Revolt. The Persians failed and made a second attempt a decade later, but were again defeated. Following the ousting of the Persians, various internal groups within Greece vied for power and autonomy, which lead to a series of internal wars. Despite the inevitable strain of the wars on the people and their economy, Greece managed to blossom forth. An important part of that blossoming was the appearance of Socrates, Aristotle, and Plato. As we think about the Western worldview, we cannot help but ponder these philosophers' profound and seemingly permanent influence on the Western mind.

Another great institution that arose in Athens during this time was that of democracy. After the Athenians deposed their last dictator, a series of reforms took place that reorganized the political systems into representative governance by the citizens and enshrined freedom of speech. The reforms gave the average man a power and responsibility never before seen; it set a high standard and has been an inspiration for democracies of our current times. It should be noted that Athenian democracy was not perfectly egalitarian, as only men could be counted as citizens. Generally, I believe these reforms were the tangible fruits of a growing ethos of humanism in the collective Greek psyche. The gods were great, but human beings were noble and important creatures in the universe as well.

The final chapter of the Classical period comes with the rise of the power of Macedonia through the energetic leadership of Philip II, who intended to spread Macedonian influence further afield. Philip's son, later to be known as Alexander the Great, was born into this atmosphere, and when Philip was murdered, Alexander quickly established himself as the new king. Alexander continued to pressure Greece, and eventually the Greeks agreed to ally with the Macedonians. This gave Alexander the force needed to attack the Persian Empire to the east, which he did with vigour, conquering territories as far away as Afghanistan and the fringes of India and Egypt. Alexander was never to return home. He died at the age of thirty-two in Asia, and his death marks the end of the Classical period.

The explosive force of expansion into a large empire created a counterflow that pulled previous foreign beliefs, ideas, and practices into Greek thought. This influence seems to have dulled and diffused the single-minded individualism and sense of purpose that had powered earlier periods of Greece. Richard Tarnas writes in *The Passion of the Western Mind* (1993):

> With the Hellenistic world extending all the way from the western Mediterranean to central Asia, the reflective individual of the later classical era was exposed to an enormous multiplicity of viewpoints. The initial expansion of Greek culture eastward was in time complemented by a strong influx of Oriental (from east of the Mediterranean) religious and political currents to the West ... The unprecedented cosmopolitanism of the new civilization, the breakup of the old order of small city-states, and the succeeding centuries of constant political and social upheaval were profoundly disorienting. (p. 75)

Despite this upheaval and the breakup of the old order, Greece remained prosperous and continued to make cultural advances. Notably, the works of the great Greek thinkers were collected, compiled, and edited to produce a concise body of works that were passed down through future ages.

Philosophy at this time seems to have taken a turn inward; rather than describing and theorizing on the nature of all things, the philosophies of the time turned more toward how a person should live and think. The philosophy of stoicism emphasized virtue and was somewhat indifferent to wealth and material things, except those that could serve virtue. Epicureanism focused on pleasure, though it was pleasure through peace of mind, freedom from fear and pain, and leading a simple life rather than hedonism as we understand it today. Skepticism focused on the concept of doubt. In the extreme it can mean doubting the existence of everything; more commonly, it is the questioning of beliefs in fields of religion, philosophy, and more recently, science. Of these three philosophies, skepticism is the one whose concepts remain most common in our current culture.

Sometime late in this period, or possibly early in the Roman period, came the dawn of alchemy as we know it. Maria the Jewess is sometimes referred to as the first Western alchemist. Although none of her writings survive, she is attested to by some of the later alchemists, notably Zosimos. We may not know exactly when, but we do know that Western alchemy arose in Alexandria, which had a rich mixture of Greek, Egyptian, and Jewish traditions, each with their own mysticism and magic. Adding to this mix was the more general knowledge of metallurgy and dyeing technology, which helped to ground the physical aspect of the process. The first seeds of Western alchemy had sprouted.

During this period Greece was like a rose just past its full glory, still rich and beautiful but waning in vitality and ready to be plucked. Certainly, the Romans recognized the decline, and in 146 BCE they took control of mainland Greece. In 30 BCE Cleopatra VII was defeated and Ptolemaic Egypt fell to Rome, ending the long history of Greek independence and rendering Greece a Roman province.

Rome served a number of functions in Western history: the absorption, preservation, and redistribution of Greek thought, inspiration for the foundation of later nations and empires, and advances in engineering and administration.

Due to the Roman Empire's vast extent and long endurance, the institutions and culture of Rome had a profound and lasting influence on the development of language, religion, art, architecture, literature, philosophy, law, and forms of government in the territories it governed. While much of this influence was a continuation of the groundwork laid by the Greeks, engineering and architecture were notably advanced with the development of the arch, vault, and dome. The quality of both the Roman design and their development of cement and concrete has allowed some of their construction to survive to the present. The Roman abilities with organization and administration were also impressive, allowing them to sustain a vast empire at a time when transportation and communications were basic. Notable was the development of Roman law and its subsequent influence on the legal systems of many countries to this day.

Another phenomenon of great consequence was the rise of Christianity. In the first century Christianity was merely an offshoot of Judaism, but it would become the state religion of Rome by 380 CE. This development was propelled by Christianity's swelling numbers, the conversion of Emperor Constantine I, and the adoption of the Constantine-supported Edict of Milan in 313 CE.

So much that shaped our world to this day had its roots in Classical Greece. The role Rome played was the collation, institutionalization, and distribution of the Greek achievements in Europe and the Mediterranean Basin. This was the case until the Roman Empire formally divided into Western and Eastern Empires. Around 375 CE the Migration period (also known as the Barbarian Invasions) began in Europe, where many tribes of Germanic peoples and Huns pushed into the collapsing Western Roman Empire. The Western Empire's process of collapse appears to have culminated in 476 CE with the Germanic Herulian's capture of the Ravenna capital and deposition of the emperor, thus marking the beginning of the Middle Ages. With the collapse of the Western Roman Empire, the Eastern Empire became, for a millennium, the repository of the ancient world's wisdom.

The Eastern Empire's role was significant. When the Eastern Empire was crumbling and fell to the Ottoman Empire in 1453 CE, there was an outflow of books and the migration of learned individuals to the rejuvenated West. This infused the culture of Western Europe with a wealth of carefully compiled and collated texts and educated people at a time that was instrumental to the West's development. Once again, the wisdom of the ancient world would guide the development of the evolving Western world.

One of the most influential developments to come out of later antiquity was Christianity. Its hold on the Western world was virtually absolute for at least fifteen hundred years and, though questioned in modern times, it remains strong to the present day. Not only has Christianity remained relatively strong in the West, but Western colonialism and missionary efforts have spread it around the world, and it has often been embraced en masse by cultures ill-prepared to consider it critically. There are a great many varieties of Christianity; despite the fragmentation, it remains the largest religion in the world. Claiming 31 percent of the human global population, Christianity is a species-wide phenomenon. It is so pervasive in many regions that its norms and values are fundamental cultural assumptions even among those who do not actively follow, or believe in, the tenets of the religion.

HISTORICAL PATTERNS AND CULTURAL ASSUMPTIONS

If our Paleolithic evolution formed the bedrock of human experience, then the Classical period laid the foundations of Western civilization. Technology, population, and economies had advanced, yet the Bronze Age's ideation reached its fruition in the Iron Age Classical period and set the tone for thought and culture to the present day. Only the trappings have changed.

By stepping back from history's isolated events to take a wider view of the flow, it is possible to recognize patterns. The most obvious is that, since the dawn of civilization, we have had cycles of boom and bust that have affected broad regions of the civilized world. Generally, the pattern reveals groups of interconnected cultures, or regional civilizations, that reach a zenith in their development, enter a period of crisis, and end with collapse. This is followed by what could be referred to as a Dark Age, leading to a gradual and determined rebuilding of a new civilization. In turn, this civilization evolves, peaks, and ultimately collapses.

The first collapse is posited to have come in the Neolithic, with the fall of the Danubian culture, a part of what some call Old Europe. The degree of cultural unity can be questioned, yet there appear to have been strong trade connections and a fairly homogeneous culture over a significant area of the Danube Basin. The reasons for the civilization's collapse are debatable. Around the beginning of the 3rd millennium BCE, things were falling apart. The towns were abandoned, and many never reoccupied, leaving the population reduced and dispersed. The region then appears to have been repopulated by migrating herders from the Pontic Steppes, the Proto-Indo-Europeans who went on to develop the civilizations of Europe.

The Mycenaean culture in Greece attained a high level of sophistication, yet ultimately failed with the Bronze Age collapse in the 13th and 12th centuries BCE. Yet another cycle would arise with the ascent of Greek civilization to its peak; though subsumed by the Roman Empire, it would live on until it crashed in the 6th century CE. The Europeans hunkered down through a Dark Age until they began to determinedly rebuild a new civilization, the peak of which we now have in the West.

Within these cycles of boom and bust there is another common phenomenon, the Golden Age. I would characterize a Golden Age not necessarily as a period of peace and prosperity, but rather as periods of extraordinary human progress in the fields of philosophy, literature, art, engineering, and social evolution. The Greek Classical period and the Renaissance of the early modern period were times of progress. Although these periods occurred and were important in societies other than the West, a broader question is why they happened. Or more specifically: What are the characteristics of a society that support surges of progress at a given time?

Golden Ages seem to appear at a particular point in a culture's development when that culture had survived its Dark Age and transitioned to a period of redevelopment and restructuring. The thinking at such times seems to have been more liberal and freer of some of the burdens of the traditions of earlier ages and the bureaucracy that stressed later cultural stages. I believe these psycho-spiritual elements set the stage for a burst of progress, rather than growth being tied just to peace and prosperity.

EMPIRE BUILDING AND WAR

Empire building appears to be at least as old as history. The first known incident took place in southern Egypt sometime around 3200 BCE, when a local kingdom centred in Hierapolis conquered two adjacent kingdoms and consolidated them. This was the first move in a sequence that would eventually create the Egyptian Empire. This process of conquer, consolidate, and expand appears to be a basic empire-building template. Originally, the proto-empires appear to have been somewhat localized to a geographic or cultural area. However, by the Classical Age, empires had grown to cross boundaries and cover vast culturally diverse areas.

The trend of expansion took another leap in the Age of Exploration when it became possible to do long-distance trans-oceanic voyages. Previously, most empires were concerned with contiguous land masses or relatively accessible islands. Effective ocean travel allowed for offshore islands and new continents to be attacked, colonized, and brought under the thrall of burgeoning empires. Wealth gathered from natural resource exploitation, slavery, and the acquisition of new products, foods, and knowledge fattened the coffers of the new transoceanic empires. Although the means and methods may have changed, imperialism has continued to the present time with much the same results. Through imperialism, wealth was concentrated among the already wealthy, cultural diversity was brutally reduced, and the environment was compromised—a very high cost for a very doubtful result. The best that can be said for empires is that they may have been instrumental in advancing civilization, albeit in a crude and barbaric fashion.

I believe empire building is an unfortunate residue of the process of becoming "civilized" in the late Neolithic and Bronze Age. War is inextricably entwined with, and essential to, empire building. In the Neolithic, with the coming of sedentism, there is for the first time evidence of what appears to be organized warfare. However, it is not until the introduction of metal weapons and the rise of the city-states that there is very clear evidence of organized war in the form of fortifications, purpose-built weapons, and soldiers' barracks. Thus began the age of empires, which in one form or another continues to this day, as does war.

War has evolved as we have evolved. During the Paleolithic, we were aggressive to the extent that was needed because it was adaptive. Other than perhaps driving beasts or humans off their kill, or possible mate-selection competitions, there was little to gain from conflict. This changed with the coming of civilizations, where there were gains to be had: land, food, livestock, material goods, and slaves. The opportunities drove our aggressive-defensive instincts to new heights. Civilized humans had more resources, more people, better technologies, and greater levels of organization than ever before. War as we know it arose in this period and has evolved ever since. It is yet another case of an effective survival instinct repurposed to something that became a maladaptive behaviour.

Along with the evolution of war came the evolution of the warrior. Surplus wealth generated by agriculture allowed for the reduction of hunting and the ability to have individuals dedicated to the preparation and making of war. The instincts that had been developed in the hunter—courage, cunning, and endurance—were relatively easily shifted to the warrior. A new identity, or archetype, had developed with its unique code and mystique. Where hunters would have collaborated with their fellow hunters, aggressive warriors sought positions of superiority among their group through internal competitions to gain rank and privilege. Military hierarchy evolved that was consistent with the increasing societal stratification. Making it to the top, with its attendant perks and prestige, would have been an accepted part of the game, as it is today. In the bigger picture, these armies, if properly handled, had cohesion and collective pride, which could be used to incite them into disciplined fierce aggression toward state enemies. The state would reach a place of cohesion and collective identity and use the army to protect itself and attack foreigners. A profession, identity, and archetype were born that remain to this day.

Cultural assumptions are concepts that are simply assumed to be true or normal in the collective mind of the culture. These are often so ubiquitous and accepted as to be unconscious and unquestioned. Unless we focus our perception, we generally operate under these assumptions without awareness of their existence. These assumptions have a profound effect on individual, national, and broader cultural levels. Unexplored, they are the curse of being a social animal.

The cultural assumptions of empire building and war have been etched on our psyche. Here are some notable ones.

- **The right of might:** Acceptability of the use of force to achieve material, political, or strategic advantage. In modern times, these aspirations are often spun with jargon, including pre-emptive strike, national security, or technical support. Nevertheless, the baseline is a gain for the aggressing group.

- **The cult of the warrior:** Special veneration for those who have "served" for the group or nation by making themselves the active agents of the group's aggressive initiative. It is different from the case of genuine defence of sovereignty, where there is a legitimate call for defence. This leads us to what I refer to as the Schmookler Dilemma—the inevitability of militarization when faced with military aggression (more on author Andrew Bard Schmookler in chapter 7).

- **The strong leader:** A self-sustaining doctrine that we must have a strong leader to guide and protect us. It is self-sustaining based on the millennia of leaders who have subjugated people into subordination, robbing them of self-confidence, initiative, and responsibility. In turn leaders took on those characteristics and infantilized their subjects. This dynamic is so ingrained that even in our modern educated context, non-hierarchical self-governance is difficult to sustain, even when it is made available.

- **Patriotism:** The militant expression of the need for a strong leader projected onto the individual's country, group, or race. The subjugated individuals strongly believe they must support the status quo and are prepared to give their life in its defence. The need for this belief is ironically based on the need for the protection and inclusion offered under the organization. "My country, right or wrong" is the classic expression of this conditioning. Again, this type of patriotism is not to be confused with the possible genuine need for rallying citizens for self-protection.

- **Hierarchy:** While hierarchy is a component in the social processes that evolve a civilization, it reaches a particular high state in the military. Layers and layers of superiority and subordination cement the concept of hierarchy in the minds of military personnel; it then spills over into the general population to further consolidate the state's hold on society.

- **Bigotry:** Inevitably in war and empire building, there must be objectification and bigotry. The aggressor must project the enemy as wrong, different, and/or too dangerous to be tolerated. Interestingly, once the enemy has been conquered and assimilated, they can become part of us and are no longer the enemy. The hatred of others is necessary to support their subjugation.

- **Revolutions:** Coupled with empire development are the rebellions of the conquered. For a people to successfully revolt, they must have an accepted social identity broad enough to challenge the conquering group's identity. Cohesion and numbers are important in this game. Revolutionaries can be seen as heroes or scoundrels, largely depending on who wins the game. There are two sets of assumptions at play: those who believe they have the right to dominate, and those who believe they have the right to rebel. The results of the collision between the two belief systems are usually suffering, destruction, and death.

- **Competition:** The appropriateness of competition is inherent in the imperial quest; however, it is also inherent when members of a culture believe they need to compete for social and economic gain. This belief in the right to tread over others to one's advantage is evident in many cultures, but imperialism is a shining example of it at play.

RELIGION

The advancement of organized religion throughout the historical period has contributed to the evolution and development of societies. Generally, at the beginning of the historical period, most people practised a variety of non-monotheistic religions. There were rustlings of the rise of monotheism as early as the 2nd millennium BCE, with the beginnings of Zoroastrianism. By the 1st millennium BCE, Judaism had firmly established itself as a monotheistic faith. This set the tone for the offshoots of Judaism to be monotheistic as well: Christianity, Islam, and Baha'i. Similarly in that era, Thales, the great early Greek philosopher, introduced the idea that nature was underpinned by one universal substance. While the Greeks continued to worship a pantheon of gods and goddesses, this idea of one universal substance took hold and influenced Greek intellectual thought from that point forward. With the arrival of Islam in this period and its sweep across the Middle East, North Africa, and somewhat into Europe, the entire Mediterranean Basin and Europe adhered to a monotheistic system.

An important countermovement to religion showed up in small ways in the 2nd millennium CE, with the first stirrings of atheism. By the time of the Enlightenment in 17th- and 18th-century Europe, atheism had gained considerable interest in intellectual circles and philosophers began to write on the subject. Atheism slowly increased as societies became more permissive and people had access to philosophical ideas and dialogues. Present-day estimates of atheism, lumped with agnosticism and the spiritually non-religious, make up an estimated 14 percent of the population.

There appear to be two opposing Western cultural assumptions that evolved. In one view, science and spirituality are incompatible, and the individual subscribes to one or the other. This is in keeping with our culture's black-and-white thinking. It is also consistent with the general view that religion and spirituality are the same thing, and that as religion has been demonstrated to be in error, it follows, if one pursues this line of thinking, that spirituality is also invalid. Conversely, a significant sector of the population remains religious and either rejects that their faith is in error and claims science is incorrect or finds another way to work around the perceived conflict of science and religion.

ECONOMICS

In its very broadest terms, economy is the process of gaining—or perhaps the utilization of—resources or commodities. In this sense, hunting and gathering can be considered a form of economy, the most fundamental one. This means that economies predate our species, stretching back into the mists of time. According to scholars Ramesh Manickam and Peter Watson (author of *Ideas: A History of Thought and Invention from Fire to Freud*, 2005), the history of long-distance commerce dates from circa 150,000 years ago. Trading is in our blood; as time passed, it became more complex and profoundly affected by civilization's evolution. Sedentary life would have allowed for the acquisition and storage of goods. The development of watercraft and the domestication of pack animals would have enabled an increase in trade volume and distance to markets. And society's militarization ensured goods could be protected in storage and shipping.

In addition, there would be innovations in the mechanisms of trade that ultimately led to credit and monetary systems as we know them. While the barter system of exchange might be imagined as the original form of trade, there is apparently no clear evidence of any known culture that operated exclusively on bartering. To this day, neighbours make mutually beneficial trades of goods and services. In ancient times, long-distance traders must have known they had a market at the end of their journey and that those people would have something that the trader wanted; otherwise, why make the journey? Despite this reality, most local and regional economies relied on the gift and/or credit concept. Gift economies can work with friendly local participants who respond in an appropriate manner to the giving and receiving of gifts. They work much less well with strangers or potential adversaries. Gift economies carry the potential for either creating warm social bonds or subjugating one person to another. Credit economies are more specific about what is offered and what is expected in return.

Eventually it became normal for certain measures of goods to serve as units of exchange, for instance, a specific measure of grain, salt, or textiles. This works, yet is a clumsy method and, if the wealth is to be held for longer periods, it requires proper storage. In numerous places, shells were used to represent units of wealth. In the 7th century BCE, Lydia (the ancient land of western Anatolia, extending east from the Aegean Sea) became the first to produce stamped metal coins. Coins in large numbers presented problems of bulk and security. Banks gradually came into being, and the coins were deposited in exchange for notes of credit. During the Song dynasty in China, standardized notes of credit were adopted; thus paper money was born. The idea of paper money was brought to the West through the accounts of travellers, including Marco Polo and William of Rubruck, in the 13th century CE. The adoption of the gold standard eventually began to replace the use of gold coins by providing banknotes based on a reserve of gold that the common people would never see. The gold standard held until its general dissolution by most countries after 1971; thereafter the world's currencies have been backed solely by faith in the value of that currency.

In brief, economies went from real products exchanged, either gifted or held in credit, that had value in themselves, to a medium of economic exchange that was more symbolic and based upon belief. With the coming of the credit card and sophisticated online banking services, many people no longer have a need for physical currency. This is a delicate situation where governments must uphold the stability of a monetary system that is upheld by the faith of the people. To make matters worse, Western economies, and most of the world, rely on continued growth to remain viable. This endless growth in a finite world does not bode well for future stability and security. With our present highly complex infrastructure, any major destabilization to the economy would likely be catastrophic. For now, most of us assume we can remain safe.

The evolution of economies has had other effects on our culture. These effects are so familiar to us that, although I believe they have changed us significantly, we do not notice them. Specifically, I am referring to the ability to hoard money, possessions, and resources. This capacity to hoard came with the sedentary life and was in full swing by the beginning of the historical period. The capacity to hoard any significant amount was probably limited to the elite until the Renaissance period in Europe. Around that time, the stranglehold on the peasants began to break down and a merchant middle class emerged. The middle class would grow broader and the elite wealthier over time until the present, with its large middle class and an elite with vast wealth. From early history to the late middle ages, wealth was associated with the "high-born," who was considered a finer person than the peasant, thus setting up an association of wealth with the quality of the holder. As the feudal system broke down, anyone could aspire to wealth and the associated prestige and refinement. A myth was born: To be rich was to be a fine person.

Becoming rich brought power and an increase in power brought gain: Wealth begets wealth. In addition, there was the opportunity to become influential in the society's power structures. Positions of power could be bought. Loans—and, of course, bribes—could secure favours. Military muscle could be hired for protection or to advance one's interests. And there was the prestige in having a kind of "muscle" that comes with wealth.

Wealth had many advantages and became desirable for its own sake—the very definition of success. Who became wealthy and how varied over time, from the inheritance of land titles and other material riches to bettering one's situation through effort and intelligence. The latter, the so-called self-made man, has become something of a cultural myth in that it is unthinkable for someone to make profit without resources, markets, labour, and infrastructure. In actuality, the self-made individual simply recognizes and pursues an opportunity, laudable perhaps, yet hardly self-made.

Wealth for many has become a virtue in itself; the successful are admired and the less successful are pitied or, worse, held in contempt. This attitude has led to a strong tendency for individuals to acquire and hoard far beyond their needs. The underlying assumption seems to be that with more wealth you will become a better, more influential, and happier person. While the quality of a person's character is subjective, assuming it can be assessed, there is nothing I have seen that suggests increased wealth correlates to increased quality of life. Yes, wealth can make a person more influential if they choose to use their wealth that way. Happiness is more complicated. Research has shown that once a person has reached a certain level of financial security and material wealth, any additional wealth has little or no effect of increasing happiness. This was strikingly demonstrated to me as a young man when I was on one of the outer islands of Fiji. The people were poor by our standards and yet friendly, generous, and apparently happy with their lot. Perhaps living in a tropical paradise had something to do with it, but I am convinced it was the fact that they had enough materially and had a great deal socially. Past a certain threshold, wealth cannot buy happiness, nor can it buy love—all it can buy is things.

And in the West, we do like our things. Our material possessions show status, provide convenience, and give us control over our environment. Ironically, this does not make us happy. A shocking 6 to 7 percent of North Americans are clinically depressed at any given time. Materialism, like money, past a certain point, does not offer a fair return. I believe we have mined out the materialistic approach; it has failed to deliver as promised. So, why do we believe and pursue it? This is a somewhat complex question. First, there are huge economic forces at play and any serious moves away from consumerism could devastate our economy. Then there is our conditioning through advertising and peer pressure. Further, there is something of an addictive quality; addiction attempts to meet a need with an unsuitable substitute that creates the momentary illusion of satisfaction, yet it quickly subsides and requires another substitute "fix." The new possession assuages my longing for a while, but then I need another possession to re-create the feeling of satisfaction. This cycle supports materialism and perpetuates the myth of the need for as much wealth as possible.

To sum up, we have a global economy, based on faith and sustained by consumerism and growth. It is perpetuated by the need to supply necessities to a growing population and the desire for unnecessary possessions and non-material perceived benefits. Being a part of this system means it is desirable to gain and hold as much wealth as possible. It is an open-ended, growth-based economy that takes a huge amount of energy and resources from the environment and locks a significant portion of it away as hoarded wealth. This system also degrades and depletes the environment, and at some point, this depletion will collide with our expanding population and consumptive economy to ensure chaos.

I believe the following Western cultural assumptions are unsustainable:

- that money is real and tangible, when in fact, the value of money depends upon faith or belief that it has tangible value as a means of exchange;
- that a successful person can be "self-made," when in fact, we are all embedded in an interdependent economic matrix; even hunter-gatherers relied on each other for survival;
- that sustained growth and increased wealth are possible, which is quite irrational given dwindling resources and ever-increasing demands for those resources;
- that wealth brings happiness, which implies that the influence and prestige wealth can bring are worth pursuing; and
- that the "playing field" is sufficiently level, which implies that, if someone has little wealth, it is really their fault for not applying themselves and bettering their situation.

END OF AN ERA

The cultural assumptions described above are only a few of those found in Western society that are contributing to our unsustainable future. Morality, misogyny, hierarchy, and adversarial politics are some others. Cultural assumptions and beliefs are what constitute overall culture. They include anything that is assumed true in our culture yet not concretely verified—things we have simply chosen to believe. While not everyone may subscribe to such assumptions, there are many who do, which in turn perpetuates and confines our cultural thought and behaviour. In select cases, cultural assumptions perpetuate unpleasant institutions: war, bigotry, and colonialism. Other assumptions are less harmful but nevertheless tend to be held unconsciously and therefore unquestioningly. This lack of awareness and curiosity tends to stabilize the culture, but it also impedes investigation and innovation at a time when radical change is required.

Our species has arrived at the end of an era and at a crisis point in our evolution; we cannot afford to simply run on old unconscious assumptions and beliefs. We must consciously examine and assess our assumptions and beliefs with an eye on our culture's future and the kind of world we seek to create. We need to cultivate a new set of beliefs based on reason, compassion, and responsibility. We need a new worldview, not naive primitive assumptions and beliefs now proven maladaptive. In the following chapters, I offer a possible worldview and the supporting rationale.

Chapter Five

The New Alchemy

WHAT IS THE NEW ALCHEMY?

In the eyes of a variety of modern esoteric and neo-Hermetic practitioners, alchemy is primarily spiritual. In this interpretation, transmutation of lead into gold is presented as an analogy for personal transmutation, purification, and perfection. Like science, alchemy was an orderly, self-contained, and self-consistent theory of the nature of things. Notwithstanding its value as a learning process in many areas of science at that time, it was in error on the physical nature of things. In the arena of physical knowledge, alchemy has rightly been displaced by modern science. However, in that displacement process, some aspects of considerable value were lost. Self-awareness, spirituality, metaphysics, ethics, and aesthetics have become peripheral to mainstream education; in the ancient alchemical tradition, these disciplines were considered essential to the pursuit of knowledge. These aspects have today become a matter of personal interest rather than a cornerstone of a well-educated individual. This may be sufficient to maintain our culture and advance science, but I question whether we are educating for wisdom.

What I refer to as "the new alchemy" introduces an alternative worldview that I believe will better support us to transition through the coming epochal shift into a more loving, creative, and sustainable future. It offers an alternative way to view four of the great relationships that constitute our lives: relationship to self, others, nature, and the cosmos. The new alchemy offers non-traditional values around societal goals, ethics, and our species' purposes. It is an attempt to rethink who, why, and what we are as humans and to look at a major redesign of our thinking and being.

In the new alchemy, I have maintained some aspects of its ancient predecessor, extending it beyond physical science while attempting to align it with that science. I have also retained the intangible elements of reality, their meaning and purpose, to provide a full-spectrum theory of life, nature, and the cosmos. The theory of the new alchemy, much like the archaic form, is based on the idea that individuals can change and develop and, through that process, can effect change in the world in which they live. By successfully modifying aspects of the external world, people validate their mastery and learn more about themselves and their world. This dialectic cycle of development—create changes in the world, and then in turn the changed world effects change in the changer—is the principle behind all alchemy, old and new. This had long been known to the authentic practitioners of old, although their focus was more on the advancement of the alchemist, whereas ours must be focused on the advancement of the species. This shift of focus constitutes one of the major differences between the old alchemy and the new.

In his 1931 book *The Hermetic Tradition*, Julius Evola refers to the old alchemy as a royal art, contrasting this to the concept of a sacred art. He appears to have used the term *royal* synonymously with the term *heroic*, focusing on individual attainment for its own sake. While both the sacred and heroic paths seek spiritual wisdom, the sacred path is more passive and communal, characterized generally by being congregational, devotional, and appeasing, whereas the heroic is more assertive, seeking individual attainment.

The new alchemy is what I refer to as a true heroic path, focusing as much on the betterment of the species as it does on the gains of the individual. Although less individualistic in its goals, it still focuses on the development of the individual through personal endeavours. However, there is no specific dogma to follow or hierarchy to join and no guarantee of success or safety along the way. This style of the heroic path seeks to empower the individual to achieve a state of personal integration wherein they have the capacity to transmute despair, pain, and ennui into purpose, joy, love, and creativity.

Many of us are committed to a peaceful, loving, and sustainable global societal emergence. Our species is generally of goodwill. If we felt otherwise about life and each other, we would never have survived the rigours of the evolutionary process. I believe we have the creative potential to identify the opportunities and effectively address the challenges that lie before us. The very fact of our survival is compelling evidence of our ability to rise to the occasion in the face of adversity; this would not be the first time we have faced an evolutionary crisis and passed the test.

THE PRINCIPLES

The new alchemy, like all theories, rests on certain principles and assumptions. The following is a brief overview of the central ideas.

The Positive Ideal

A foundational assumption and guiding principle of the new alchemy is the idea that, despite whatever neurosis, vanity, or compensation an individual possesses, most humans seek a better future where society is more loving, creative, and sustainable and is free from the atrocities of war, gross socio-economic inequality, and environmental degradation. Many people are caught in ignorance or consumed by their own narcissistic desires. Nevertheless, beneath these petty human foibles there is a greater dignity and desire. In no small measure, the intention of the new alchemy is to awaken this dignity and desire and call it forth into action in the world.

Spirituality

Once generally a synonym for *religion*, the modern usage of the term *spirituality* has grown to be more inclusive. While religion is a particular expression of spirituality, I define spirituality more generally as an individual's relationship to the intangibles of life: purpose, love, origin, nature of the universe, and the divine. When I speak of the divine, I am referring to the loving, creative intelligence of the cosmos—what many people refer to as God. Generally, spirituality is our relationship and beliefs about the unknown, mysterious, or subjective nature of things that cannot be adequately explained by reason or measured by a known scale.

Personal experience and the study of human evolution have drawn me to the conclusion that within all human beings there is an innate spiritual urge or impulse. We want to understand who we are, how the world works and why, and what the meaning of it all is. Since ancient times, we have practised intentional burial, which presupposes an afterlife or some kind of honouring of this life; when we were still scrabbling for survival, we took time to paint and carve sacred symbols. Amazingly, before we mastered agriculture, we had built our first temple—not simply a pile of stones but the magnificent beauty and intricate detail of Göbekli Tepe (9500–8000 BCE). Through late prehistory and the historic period, some of the greatest and most inspiring architecture has been of a religious nature. Spirituality has found expression across the globe in all cultures and in all times.

In current times, the undeniable success of science and its tendency toward skepticism has collided with the stubborn literalism of most religions. As science has shown the literal interpretation of most holy books to be in error, many people have trivialized, denied, or lapsed into confusion about the great questions of life. Such a polarization on the issue of spirituality and the denial of our authentic nature has not served individuals or our society well. Many of the great human achievements have occurred in a context of spiritual freedom. An openness, tolerance, and acceptance of our nature and the beliefs of others will better support us to face the coming changes.

It's All Love
Love, at the cosmic level, is what gave rise to consciousness and energy, the two primal forces whose separation and reunion were responsible for the Big Bang and the formation of the universe. Love, in this cosmic sense, is a more vast and majestic force than what we think of as love on the human scale. It appears to be a profound longing to become, a desire for manifestation, and a calling forth of creative potential from whatever mystery preceded space-time into all that it is now and continues to become. Although evolutionary cosmologist Brian Swimme does not speak of it in these terms, his documentary *Journey of the Universe* (journeyoftheuniverse.org), co-written with historian Mary Evelyn Tucker, presents a description of the evolution of the universe that goes beyond the mechanistic and suggests a mystery that could be described as love.

Human love, even in its highest form, is just a tiny holographic splinter of cosmic love, and it has been shaped and coloured by the immense challenge of incarnation. Most notable of the changes wrought by incarnation is the introduction of love's paradoxical counterpart, fear—the instinct to preserve. The forces we perceive as divine manifest on an incredible scale, with exquisite elegance, and operate beyond fear in a state of pure becoming.

Spirit in All Things

If all things ultimately are the descendants of cosmic energy and cosmic consciousness, then it follows that all things, whether we see them as "alive" in a strict sense or not, are imbued with divine essence and could be seen as having spirit. This idea is common in numerous pagan mythologies including Hermeticism, and to a small extent in Christianity. Although there is no scientific evidence to discredit it, the concept of spirit in all things has not generally been supported by the scientific community.

Intention and the Cosmic Challenge

I believe the unfolding universe has purpose, that intention is embedded in the order underlying all manifestation, and that the intention is ultimately focused on the perfect synthesis of consciousness and energy as expressed in a concretely manifested form—the most sophisticated expression of spirit in matter and matter inspired. The purpose is not immediately clear; however, the evidence provided by our senses and by advanced scientific instruments leads me to believe the unfolding has a direction. When one looks at the history of the universe, the evolution of life, and the trajectory of civilization, the intention of the cosmos appears to favour increasingly complex, dynamic forms and interrelated systems that are sufficiently stable to support growth and change.

If we are part of an intention greater than ourselves and choose to play a conscious, active part in that unfolding, we need to accept that we are presented with what I refer to as the "cosmic challenge," which is to align ourselves with divine cosmic love and through our actions contribute to the unfolding and evolution of life. Accepting that there is a greater intention to the universe points to the purpose of life for self-aware creative forms and imparts a passion for fulfilling this purpose.

Paradox

There is an ancient question about whether humanity is one unified manifestation or an agglomeration of many separate individuals. The answer is yes to both, which is a paradox. In this case the use of the term *paradox* refers to (per the Cambridge online dictionary) "a situation or statement that seems impossible or is difficult to understand because it contains two opposite facts or characteristics." *Paradox* describes many situations in the world where two apparently logically inconsistent states are true and sustained over time and no amendment to theory or reality is considered appropriate.

The discomfort of accepting paradox comes from our limitations in interpreting our perceptions, specifically, the linear and polarized style of our common thinking. Logic suggests we look at a question and progress through a series of linear conceptual steps until we reach the one right answer. This is an old tradition in the West that reaches back to the early Greek philosophers, and in many ways it has served us well. However, it does not always apply, and efforts to force a true paradox into a single answer or truth results in a denial of one side of the paradox. Doing so makes the world simpler, more manageable, and smaller in a figurative sense. However, in denying paradox, we sacrifice mental flexibility, resilience, and adaptability—the important capabilities we require to face pending rapid and radical change.

As Within, So Without

The concept "as within, so without," which is consistent with the old alchemical idea "as above, so below," is critical in bringing the ideals of the new alchemy to bear in the practical world. The principle is self-similarity, where each stratum consists of a set of smaller, discrete units distinctly similar to, yet not the same as, the stratum above.

A simplified description of the universe might be:

- solar systems are smaller self-similar units to galaxies,
- planets and their moons are similarly related to the solar systems,
- the whirling patterns of fluid systems are related to planets and moons, and
- those patterns are similar to the whirling electron fields.

Each stratum is a descent into smaller forms that carry the heritage of the larger form. Therefore, active self-aware beings who wish to create change in the social stratum in which they live need to cultivate that change within themselves to create the resonance of change outside themselves. For example, if we wish increased peace in the world, we should look to increased peace in our hearts.

Self-Compassion and Compassion

The process of socialization appears to leave most of us with some residue of insecurity, self-doubt, and negative self-judgment, if not outright self-hate. This inner condition detrimentally affects both the individual and society. The individual can suffer, consciously or not, from lack of confidence, indecision, irrational fear, depression, self-loathing, or addiction, along with other conditions. Not only does this suffering reduce joy and success in an individual's life, but it impedes their productivity and creative potential, thus robbing society of their gifts and abilities. But this effect is not what has the greatest negative impact on society.

Psychological projection is a mechanism where an individual, or society, attributes their own thoughts, feelings, or behaviours to another person or group. The term is most commonly used to describe defensive projection—attributing one's own unacceptable urges to another. This is true of issues involving self-worth and self-loathing, as well as many other disowned and undesirable aspects of the inner self. Thus, if we are prone to loathe ourselves and find fault within, we will deny the issue within ourselves and project it onto others. Simply put, to hate within makes it far more likely we will hate without. This mechanism, coupled with ignorance, plays a major role in the formation of blame, separation, and bigotry in our societies.

Fortunately, there is an antidote to this toxin that may be gleaned from the simple wisdom of the maxim "as within, so without." An important component that embodies the principle is that of compassion. If we change the inner consciousness, we change the inner experience as well as the outer behaviour. While the release from self-criticism and fear has profound benefits for the individual and society, it is not an easy undertaking. It is a formidable challenge to unpack and integrate the negative aspects of our socialization; old patterns die hard and only through diligent efforts. However, the result is a shift to a happier, more creative, and more loving individual, which in turn brings about a healthier, more productive society.

Solve et Coagula

Underpinning growth and change on virtually every level of manifestation is the old alchemical principle of *solve et coagula*, which roughly translates as "to dissolve and to coagulate." This process of something coming apart and recombining to create something new is seen at every level of the physical world. The explosion of a dying star creates more complex elements than originally existed (nucleogenesis), where the elements recombine to create new molecules, which in turn break down and re-form anew. Our biosphere systems use the principle of death and renewal both in the reproduction and decomposition processes. This principle also extends into our emotional lives, in terms of how we preserve or end relationships to create new ones.

The concept of breaking down and recombining can be extended to our intellectual world, where ideas become outmoded and fall apart only to have elements of those ideas revived and revised into a new concept or theory. The fundamental process of dissolution and creative recombination adds complexity and vitality to manifestation and is continuously at work in our individual lives, in the evolution of the species, and through all levels of the universe.

Four Aspects and Four Relationships

The four aspects refers to four principal divisions of the human experience: the body, emotions/unconscious (heart), conscious mind/intellect, and spirit. The four relationships refer to the individual human's relationship with themselves, other humans, nature, and the divine (the mystery, the unknown, God, or whatever one cares to call it).

The body's nature and structure is well understood and obvious. The emotions/unconscious is more complex; it encompasses both our consciously experienced emotions and our unconscious processes and drivers. The conscious mind/intellect is what many identify with as "me." Lastly, and most controversially, is the spirit. The human spirit, as I define it, is greater than the individual and is the presence of the collective human consciousness in the individual's subconscious. The human spirit anchors us in the unseen structures of what it is to be human; through the human collective consciousness, we ultimately connect with the cosmic consciousness. In a manner of speaking, it is what makes individual humans more than the sum of their parts.

Our relationship to ourselves is generally taken for granted, as most people assume they know themselves. However, without considerable focused effort, self-awareness is not achievable.

Most of us are driven by unconscious processes, in denial of our inner conflicts and habitual mental habits, living our lives in something of a trance. Genuine self-knowledge can be the most liberating and empowering process one can undertake. "Know thyself" is truly a key maxim on the route to our greatest positive potential. A second major key to unlocking our internal relationship is the development of self-compassion. A healthy feeling of self-worth—reasonable expectations of oneself and self-acceptance—is essential to an authentic, stable, and happy relationship with self.

Our relationship with others is both important and complex. It requires an interaction of two complicated psychic systems, each with its unique unconscious processes, denials, and inner conflicts layered onto preconceptions and expectations of the other. Therefore, although self-knowledge is important, it must be coupled with knowledge of the general human experience. One needs to extend compassion to others and develop skills of interrelated connection: communication, boundaries, and authenticity. Developing successful relationships with others is more difficult than many think. Few recognize the conscious effort needed to acquire the knowledge and skills necessary for meaningful sharing, which undoubtedly accounts for many difficult and failed relationships.

Generally, a relationship with nature is often easier and less demanding than a relationship with ourselves and others. Nature offers us nearly endless possibilities of learning that can be rich and rewarding, because it brings us into more direct contact with the manifested evidence of the energies and consciousness of the divine.

Even if one chooses to believe there is no universal formative energy, it is universally necessary for human beings to have a concept of how the universe works. Although we reach conclusions about the nature of the universe that are impossible to prove or disprove, we still seek to develop explanations. Like all the relationships mentioned, the relationship to the divine forces, or the mystery, or whatever it is you perceive it to be, is richest when approached with consciousness, compassion, and openness.

The Myth of Rationality

Since Descartes, the mind and rationality have been held as ideals; the body is a vehicle, and the heart has been subordinated to the educated and evolved mind. In many cases, the confirmed rationalist rejects the idea of spirit and attempts to explain the human experience with reason. I believe this to be a serious self-deception. We are not rational beings, but beings capable of rationality. Unless the other aspects are integrated and balanced, alleged reason is little more than rationalization, a justification of the needs and desires that arise from unconscious drives and emotions.

Life evolved as an interactive dialogue to bring about the most likely group survival. As the bodies of life forms evolved, they were compelled to add both neural and vascular components to the conversation in the quest for survival. These were the primitive building blocks of what we call body, mind, and heart. These components are now called upon, as they always have been, to develop unified, functional, and adaptive creatures. There are no superior components, only beings better adapted to survive. The thinking mind is precious, but only in the context of a balanced and integrated whole.

Transmutation

Fundamental to alchemy is the concept of transmutation: the idea that a human being, through knowledge, skill, and practices, can achieve changes in the basic nature of things. For the alchemists of old, this meant changes both within the individual and in the external material world. In the new alchemy, we are concerned with transmutations within the practitioner and the non-material aspects of the outer world. Our desired outcome is the refinement and development of the practitioner, so they can contribute positively to their own transmutation and that of the larger collective.

Basically, the internal transmutations of a new alchemist are focused on turning the negative aspects, beliefs, and habits of the self into their positive counterparts. Possibly the most primal and prominent transmutation is that of fear to love, and closely related, of hatred to compassion. Even limited success of these two transmutations will change the practitioner's perception of self, others, and their world, as well as their relationships and their society.

Potentially, even more transformational for the individual is the transmutation of the personal shadow (the self's emotional blind spot—the part the ego does not want to acknowledge) into the light of consciousness. Bringing the material of the shadow into awareness enables us to achieve a choice point from which numerous outcomes are possible. Surprisingly, it is within the shadow that we find some of the most brilliant, creative elements of ourselves. Carl Jung, the famous psychologist, spoke frequently about the shadow and suggested that behind its seemingly irredeemable face lies the very key to continued individuation. Not everything we find in our shadow is brilliant and creative. In such cases, it is wise to bring these shadow aspects into one's conscious state, accept the shadow's reality, and hold it in one's heart with self-compassion.

According to Jung, there is also the great transmutation of the polarized self-perception as being either one sex or another into a more unified self-concept, or to use Jung's words, the integration of the anima and animus within the individual. This act is closely related to integrating the shadow and ultimately produces an individual with a more complete, balanced, and stable sense of self. It also contributes to holding all others in compassion, regardless of their gender or partner preference. In short, it produces a more whole person, which is why I believe the symbol of the hermaphrodite had such prominence in alchemy: it was understood that sexual integration is of great importance to the individual's growth.

Although I believe the three transmutations of fear to love, shadow to consciousness, and sexual polarization to integration are the most important, there are numerous others that contribute to the evolution of consciousness. They might include the transmutations of misfortune into opportunity, self-doubt into confidence, and conflict into peace. The art of transmutation is high-order work that carries with it commensurately high rewards.

Mythical Thinking
Mythical thinking differs in several important ways from our daily conscious thinking. Although available to all, it requires focused effort to develop the conscious capacity to think mythically. The closest most of us come to connecting with our mythic story is either by reading myths themselves or through our dreams. It is a less personal level of thought, where one is more likely to see the self as a symbol in a timeless drama of existence rather than perceiving it as a singularity at the centre of one's experience. Our personal mythology is a deep force within us that shapes our destiny, and just as we are driven by our emotions, we are driven by our personal myths. A conscious understanding of them supports us to work with these powerful inner forces and achieve mastery in our lives. Engaging with the concepts of archetypes and mythemes can enhance and refine our mythological knowledge.

An archetype is a generalized template, or script, of a character role, such as Mother, Father, Warrior, or Priest. Our fundamental archetypes develop at a very early stage of life, well ahead of rational thought. The archetype becomes a general role adopted by the child as a response to their environment and evolving sense of self derived from pre-logical associative and magical thinking. In this process, each individual takes the archetypal template and customizes it to their circumstances and temperament, thereby developing a version of that archetype that is as unique to them as a thumbprint. By the time this process is substantially complete, our archetypes are deeply set, generally unconscious, and very hard, if not impossible, to change.

Mythemes are related but distinct. Rather than being a psychic template, a mytheme is a template for a human experience or circumstance. In the human collective unconscious, there are generalized templates or scripts for the situations that humans experience. The morality play, the hero's journey, the revolution, and the struggle to individuate are all examples of mythemes.

Groups, nations, and cultures are driven by mythologies of which they lack conscious awareness. National mythologies are significant factors driving us to war and the oppression of others. Awareness of archetypes, particularly our personal archetype(s), and the common mythemes of our species enables us to view ourselves objectively. The capacity to think in mythical terms allows us to examine ourselves and the groups, nations, and cultures in which we are embedded. Rather than being caught up in our individual challenges in life, we can view the situation from a larger perspective, which empowers us to make decisions and initiate actions that are based on a conscious understanding of our motivations.

Primary Politics
"Primary politics" is the term I use to describe fundamental attitudes and prejudices laid down in our early development phase,

possibly from the last trimester through to about the sixth year. These early beliefs are primitive answers to such questions as: Is the world a safe place? Am I worthy? Are women, or men, good or bad? The beliefs are established and anchored in the pre-logical phase and based on the child's limited life experience. The critical factor is that these beliefs are generally unconscious and deeply entrenched. They follow us throughout our lives and unknowingly colour our interactions and responses to the world. Although it is usually not difficult to bring these persistent prejudices and attitudes to a conscious level, it is a challenging task to bring them under control. However, once this is achieved, our ability to be free, wise, and compassionate is enhanced.

Enlightenment

The process of enlightenment is a journey—a movement along a continuum that has no end. However, there is a milestone on the journey so profound as to appear as an ultimate endpoint: the mastery of fear and the triumph of love. This is not a cessation of the experience of fear or a withdrawal from life. Rather, it is the capacity to be fully engaged, conscious, and aware of what motivates our actions so we can make choices that are based on love rather than unconscious fears. This is a path of profound significance, with the potential, if enough of us pursue it, to shift the evolution of our future.

THE PRACTICE

The practice of the new alchemy is aimed at developing the potential of individuals in all four aspects to enable a rich personal life and serve the epochal shift. As the individuals within a society evolve, so does the society. The ultimate vision is the realization of a more loving, creative, and sustainable world.

Worldview

To live a rich, creative, and loving life, one must cultivate a worldview that is self-aware, open, positive, and compassionate. There are many and varied ways to support the development of a positive, successful worldview: education, personal development, spiritual pursuits, travel outside of one's culture, and experiences in nature. These endeavours can contribute to informing and enriching our worldview; however, the most important attribute is the willingness to open our hearts and minds to change in our dialogue with life.

We have a greater need for open flexibility than ever before. The systems we have used in the past are failing, and we must move toward radical change. The focus of the new alchemy is to encourage thought, dialogue, and connection, to question certainty and induce greater openness and curiosity about alternative concepts.

Political and social change arises when a significant number of people evolve a modified worldview and exert their influence to initiate change. The awakened individual promotes political and social activities in the best interest of humanity and the planet. A positive, loving worldview is the keystone of adaptability, progress, and real sustainability.

Personal Development

We but mirror the world. All the tendencies present in the outer world are to be found in the world of our body. If we could change ourselves, the tendencies in the world would also change. As a man changes his own nature, so does the attitude of the world change towards him. This is the divine mystery supreme. A wonderful thing it is and the source of our happiness. We need not wait to see what others do.
—Mahatma Gandhi, 1913

If we seek societal change, the individuals within that society must embody those thoughts and actions; the shift must come from within the individuals and thereby shape the collective. As is verified through thousands of years of history, it will not come from "great individuals." Those who wish to lead will learn to follow the impetus of the evolving shift and step up to serve. However, the core and initiating essence of this process is our own internal shift and its subsequent behavioural shift.

An internal shift begins with seeking self-awareness—a process of learning about our early development and subsequent life experiences, and how they have shaped our beliefs, attitudes, character, and ultimately our behaviour. Individuals, along with our species, have maladaptive coping strategies that are imprinted from our childhood. It is no small undertaking to learn of our unconscious drives and amend them. As we gain self-awareness, we become more aware of our fellow travellers and evolve a greater compassion for ourselves and others.

While self-awareness is critical to personal development, attitudes of tolerance, curiosity, egalitarianism, and openness are essential. Presence, equanimity, kindness, and focus are some of the characteristics of a well-developed individual. The range of skills one can develop is huge and varied, sweeping from the esoteric and intellectual to the mundane and physical. One of the foremost abilities of an evolving individual is a capacity to remain stable in difficult or rapidly changing situations, and by accepting the situation's reality, to transmute it to its best possible positive form.

Out in the World
Living in community is our natural state; we are social animals. Through most of our evolution, we have relied on our interdependence with others in our tribe for survival. As a result,

we have evolved with a need for community at both the physical and psycho-emotional levels. Social psychology researcher James S. House (in *Psychosomatic Medicine*, 2001) says: "The magnitude of risk associated with social isolation is comparable with that of cigarette smoking and other major biomedical and psychosocial risk factors" (quoted on Wikipedia). Social isolation is a condition we must take seriously. Being part of a community that is diverse and cohesive enough to allow us to grow, and to give and receive nourishment, is what supports us to become our best selves.

In a similar fashion to community, service is good for us. Studies clearly indicate there are mental health benefits associated with being of service to others, and in recent years, there has been evidence of physical benefits as well. This is no more surprising than the benefits of community, for we have been serving one another for many millennia in whatever capacity we were able or called upon to do: mother, hunter, shaman, healer. It is a natural aspect of being human. If we pursue service with a focus on another, family, our community, or some aspect of the greater world with an open heart and in a manner that lends meaning to our lives, it will bring us significant benefits.

Service in the world that is adversarial and dominance-based, where aggressive and violent actions are used to support a cause, has severe drawbacks in terms of social, economic, and environmental sustainability. What one side builds, the other seeks to tear down; the collective creativity is sundered, because of the separation caused by the contest and resulting victory or defeat.

The alternatives to the adversarial contests are collaboration and education. Similar to community and service, collaboration is an ancient human aptitude anchored in, and critical to, our long struggle for survival. While there were some contests of dominance in our Paleolithic past, the predominant mode of living within the tribe was collaborative. With the onset of civilization, dominance gradually became the primary mode of living. However, this behaviour is no longer adaptable. Many highly effective people are forging new systems of collaboration that are well suited to our modern conditions and mindset. Education is also an ancient practice that can serve our ends far more effectively than aggressive competition for dominance. If we can learn enough about a situation, we can then seek a solution that considers both or all sides of the issue without resorting to force or coercion.

The new alchemy, unlike the old, does not celebrate the achievement and advancement of the lone philosopher; it seeks a collective wisdom and collective creative effort. The role of the individual in relation to society is in the service of uniting, inspiring, and supporting the collective genius. Individuals themselves inevitably reap many benefits from the pursuit of such an ideal: self-knowledge, an understanding of life, meaning and purpose, a sense of belonging and contributing, and the inevitable peer recognition. Such benefits bring the practitioner a sense of peace, fulfillment, and satisfaction. The process informs and nourishes both society and the individual's dynamic interdependent relationships.

Meaning and Purpose

At some point most of us ask ourselves: What am I doing here? What is life about? What is my purpose? This is a natural situation for a self-conscious creature. Once our bellies are full and there is no immediate danger, we humans try to make sense out of life. Yet, regardless of our wisdom and maturity, such questions often lack rational answers.

At least since the Axial Age (circa 800 to 200 BCE) proposed by Karl Jaspers, humans have been trying to find rationally based answers to the "Ultimate Question of Life, the Universe, and Everything" (as Douglas Adams's *Hitchhiker's Guide* famously puts it). From that time to the present moment, no one has succeeded in providing a generally accepted answer. Modern science, powerful as it is, has not proved adequate to this challenge. Even if we set aside the scientific principle that states science or any other system of knowledge cannot know anything absolutely and completely, there is another issue with attempting to seek rational answers. Science's great strength is in dealing with the physical world, where postulates can be readily measured, tested, and described in rational systems. The great questions of life are not like this; they are subjective, mutable, and context based. It comes down to a personal choice. We can seek meaning through religious adherence, claim (despite evidence to the contrary) that reason and science have found the answer, or accept living in the tension of not knowing.

Alternatively, we can devise our own belief system. The search for meaning is one of personal choice, and we should seek answers that best serve us. As there is no knowing in this matter, we have the freedom to choose. By the same token, we can never know if the belief system we have chosen is true or accurate, and therefore, it should be held lightly. The key to achieving personal well-being is through diligently seeking meaning and purpose, while making choices that are appropriate in terms of context, temperament, and needs.

Materialism
In the pursuit of personal development, we discover that we have needs and that unnecessary denial of genuine needs is unhealthy and potentially debilitating. Furthermore, compensating for denied needs leads to discontent, and one of the most deceptive and treacherous forms of discontent is seeking compensations through materialism.

Materialism in this context is the acquisition of wealth and/or property beyond reasonable need or use. Like many compensations, materialism does not satisfy the need other than providing a temporary experience of the need being met. The experience is fleeting, and more of the compensatory substance must be acquired. There is never enough.

Materialism is deceptive, almost indefinable, for a variety of reasons. What is too much? It is perfectly reasonable to desire sufficient wealth and possessions to live a comfortable, secure life, but at some point, the desire for acquisition becomes neurotic. We have an ancient predisposition to acquire resources when available—a once adaptive instinct that now works against our best interests. Gluttony, particularly in the West and increasingly in other cultures, contributes to global climate change, creates waste, consumes resources, and preys upon the less privileged for their labour. In short, it is damaging our biosphere and threatening our future.

Right Livelihood

Related to what and how much we consume, or hoard, is the question of what we do to get it. Our complex, diverse, and multilayered modern culture gives individuals a myriad of opportunities and occupational choices. Beyond parental or peer pressure, the choice of how to earn a living is essentially left to the individual. There are many factors to consider: interests, aptitude, life goals, remuneration. The conscious person also includes deliberations on how their life decisions may contribute to, or detract from, the species and the planet. This is now more important than ever.

Reproduction

Another critically important lifestyle question for our time is that of reproduction. Like other significant issues we face, it has its roots in our ancient drive to survive; our survival both on the individual and species levels was linked to successful reproduction. Although natural, the drive to reproduce has become a major threat. There are many different estimates of the maximum sustainable human population, but there is general agreement that we have already exceeded what can be sustained in the long term. The 2022 "Scientists' Warning on Population," published in the journal *Science of the Total Environment*, states that "environmental analysts regard a sustainable human population as one enjoying a modest, equitable middle-class standard of living on a planet retaining its biodiversity and with climate-related adversities minimized," which is estimated at between two and four billion people. The overpopulation issue underpins, in one way or another, almost every critical issue of our time. As much as it pains us to accept its reality, we must face this issue.

A good deal of noble effort has gone into population controls, yet we remain woefully short of a sustainable solution. The common thought in Western culture at this time seems to be that a couple should have two children, thus reproducing themselves and ensuring population maintenance. This would have been an impactful strategy several generations ago, when Western families were typically much larger, but now more stringent measures are required to avert a deepening crisis. If we do not voluntarily reduce our population, it is inevitable that nature will achieve that objective for us. The consequences of the latter, in terms of human suffering and environmental degradation, are horrific. It is the responsibility of every self-aware individual to make life decisions in support of a gentle reduction in global population. We are social animals on a finite planet, and we must accept that our individual actions have an impact far beyond ourselves.

THE OBJECTIVE OF EVOLUTION

All of the factors discussed in this chapter point toward one objective: to pursue personal development and self-awareness in order to enrich lives and contribute to the evolution of our species. I believe our survival, and the evolution of our future, depends on this objective becoming a focus for humankind. It is through this process that we will build a society of sufficient strength and flexibility to absorb the shocks of the coming epochal shift.

Chapter Six

The Cosmology

I am not a cosmologist. What I am offering is an overview of the generally accepted facts of the origin and nature of our cosmos followed by thoughts on what preceded the Big Bang, along with my interpretations. It is worth noting that not all scientists agree on the big picture or the fine points on the nature of the cosmos. As in other fields of science, there is critical debate on many points, which is an indication of a healthy inquiry process.

ORIGINS

A Sketch of Cosmic Evolution

Primordial: What preceded the Big Bang and occurred in the very earliest moment in the life of the universe (the Planck epoch) is currently considered unknowable. This is reasonable, given that any set of physical laws, such as the theory of general relativity, would not serve to explore an era when space-time reality had not yet formed. Thus, the essential origin of the universe remains a subject of keen interest, debate, and conjecture.

By the end of the Planck epoch, things become more comprehensible, and it is generally believed that gravity separated from the other fundamental interactions. At this point, the fundamental physical laws that define today's reality were not yet formed. All that existed was a super-dense, super-hot, undefined primal reality. The universe expanded at extreme speed and began to cool sufficiently to enable a complex series of subatomic processes. Forces of interaction separated; subatomic particles formed, split, and collided with one another to annihilate each other or fuse into something new (the alchemical term *solve et coagula* could be used to describe this fusion). These processes would evolve until the first hydrogen and helium atoms were formed, 379,000 years after the initial event. This ended the Primordial era of the development of the universe.

Stelliferous: The presence of stable hydrogen atoms ushered in the Stelliferous era—the era of the stars. The intense processes of joining and splitting would continue, as gravity began to pull hydrogen atoms into clouds, and those clouds formed clusters that in turn gave birth to the first stars between 100 and 150 million years after the Big Bang. With this development, the cosmic union had brought forth its first "children" in the form of stable, long-term processes that continue as part of our current physical reality.

The great progression of evolution, or the divine becoming, had begun from an inconceivable singularity to a frenzy of subatomic interactions, to the development of simple atoms, and then, on a grand, macro level, to the evolution of stars. However, there was a grander physical expression yet to come: the formation of billions of galaxies beginning four to five million years later. Once the galaxies were extant, the nature of those galaxies continued to evolve, with the expansion of the universe, the collisions between galaxies, and the life cycles of the stars within them. Evolving celestial bodies came into existence, each composed of millions of individual stars with their own unique characteristics.

One characteristic of stars is their metallicity: the relative number of metals in the star's chemical composition. This measure has been used to classify stars. Population 1 stars, the youngest, are metal-rich, while Population 2 stars are older with less metals. There is also a hypothetical Population 3, now extinct, made up of huge hot stars containing virtually no metals. It is thought that these primordial giants ended their lives as supernovas that created metals through the process of nucleosynthesis and spewed them into the universe. These metals were then available for the formation of Population 2 stars. Upon the demise of Population 2 stars, more metals were dispersed into the universe to facilitate the creation of metal-rich Population 1 stars. Of significance is the existence of terrestrial (rock/metal/mineral-based) planets orbiting Population 1 stars. They began to evolve about four billion years after the Big Bang and will continue to evolve for a very long time. The life cycles of these stars evolved planets with increased metals and elements, and more planets would develop with the new stars. About nine billion years after the Big Bang, a very special, at least to us, star came into existence—our Sun.

Along with the Sun, the solar system's celestial bodies evolved through a long, complex series of interactions. The most generally accepted cosmic evolutionary theory is referred to as the nebular hypothesis, in which a gravitational collapse of a molecular cloud formed a large ball of dust particles and gases. This ball began to condense and spin, probably due to the impact of a supernova's shockwave. The spinning formed the mass into a disk shape, with the greatest density in the centre. The central mass became our Sun, while the planets would accrete from collisions of particles in the outer disk. Earth and the other terrestrial planets are thought to have formed in their unique fashion due to their proximity to the Sun. Within the warmer inner or frost-free zone of the solar system, gaseous elements remained as gases, and these gaseous elements were then more readily influenced to move out toward the cooler areas of the system. In the cooler realms, they could condense and freeze into solid form, giving rise to the great ice planets, Uranus and Neptune. Most of the denser metal/mineral elements of the inner system evolved to form the rocky planets we know today. In the early stages of Earth's formation, the metallic elements became densely packed and began to melt. With the melting came the gravitational sorting of the elements, with the denser metals, primarily iron, forming the planet's molten central core. The spinning iron core established a strong magnetic field around Earth, shielding it from much of the Sun's solar radiation, a major factor in the evolution of life. Earth was in a special relationship to the Sun: neither too distant, thus becoming a gas giant, nor too close, resulting in the loss of its precious water.

The planets shifted orbital position as they developed, an event believed to have had a significant influence on the formation of the solar system. The forces that drive planetary migration are varied and complex, yet there is little doubt the interactions took place and are implicated in the development of various features of our solar system. These migrations, and their associated effects, underpin the most generally accepted theory of the origins of our moon. Referred to as the "giant impact theory," it postulates a roving Mars-sized planet impacting early Earth, blasting a large mass from both bodies. Some of this material was captured by Earth's gravity and gradually accreted into our moon. The giant impact theory, although still debated, best matches the current physical evidence and explains Earth's axial tilt, which is critical for seasonal weather dynamics. The large size of our moon also gave rise to a local tidal effect, a force significantly greater than the Sun's tidal impact. The moon's strong tidal effect governs the tides, thus creating the intertidal zones, which were of critical importance to the evolution of life. In addition, planetary migration played a large role in creating Earth's Late Heavy Bombardment, which occurred 4.1 to 3.8 billion years ago (abbreviated 4.1 to 3.8 Ga, meaning giga-annums ago). The bombardment reshaped Earth's crust and delivered water to a hot planet previously unable to retain moisture. And finally, the revised orbits of the giant gas planets (Jupiter and Saturn) and their strong gravitational forces account for a vastly reduced frequency of asteroids and comets that have an impact on the inner planets.

A Sketch of Animate Life
Very early in Earth's development (the Hadean period, 4.5 Ga), there was a planet with a solid crust, large bodies of acidic waters, high temperatures, and a toxic atmosphere. Though this does indeed sound hellish, the Hadean period was not the roiling inferno of lava and fire originally believed to have been. Some scientists have speculated that life began during this period. Although there is no undisputed proof, it is at least likely that the building blocks of life, the fundamental organic compounds, could have formed at this time. If life's evolution did begin in the Hadean, it was in for a severe test during the Late Heavy Bombardment. It is assumed that any life that may have formed would have been destroyed in this event, unless it survived around the hydrothermal vents of an ocean. Interestingly, there are many good reasons to believe those locations are where life began, whenever it began. Whatever the case, Earth took a severe pounding, apparently again rendering its surface molten. How planetary water remained under those conditions is amazing. The bombardment ended between 4 to 3.8 Ga and Earth's crust began to re-form. Whether life originated before or after the Late Heavy Bombardment has been contested by scientists, yet in terms of time, it is merely a technical point. There was in any case an amazingly short period—about 800,000 years—between the formation of Earth and the first indications of life.

For completeness, it is worth noting a recent theory describing an ultra-early origin of life in the universe. A 2013 article in *Nature* magazine ("Life possible in early Universe" by Zeeya Merali) profiles Abraham Loeb, an astrophysicist at Harvard University, who realized that in the early universe, the energy required to keep water liquid could have come from the cosmic microwave background, the afterglow of the Big Bang, rather than from host stars. Today, the temperature of this relic radiation is just 2.7 Kelvin (-270 degrees Celsius), but at an age of around fifteen million years, it would have kept the entire universe at a balmy 300K (+27°C).

Loeb states that rocky planets could have existed at that time, in pockets of the universe where matter was exceptionally dense, leading to the formation of massive short-lived stars that would have enriched these pockets with the heavier elements required to make planets. He suggests that there would have been a habitable epoch of two or three million years during which rocky planets would have been able to maintain liquid water, regardless of their distance from a star. "The whole universe was once an incubator for life," Loeb says.

Whether further scientific inquiry and debate will prove this concept true or even viable remains to be seen, yet it is an intriguing possibility. Though it has been argued that the time span at this state of the universe was too short to produce self-regenerating life, it quite possibly could have produced the complex organic building blocks of life. If this were the case, such building blocks could have been distributed through the universe very early and underpinned a type of panspermia (the idea that life has been dispersed throughout the universe via asteroids or comet).

Along the same lines, yet more demonstrable in a lab, are National Aeronautics and Space Administration experiments. In March 2015, NASA scientists reported that, for the first time, complex DNA and RNA organic compounds of life, including uracil, cytosine, and thymine, had been formed under outer space conditions. This strongly suggests Earth's biosphere might not be the only environment suitable for the evolution of life's building blocks. Then there is the concept of panspermia. Not only is it possible to create organic chemicals in space, but modestly complex terrestrial life forms have shown the capacity to survive unprotected in the harsh environment of space. This being the case, it is not inconceivable that life itself was transported to Earth, perhaps during the Late Heavy Bombardment.

Quite a few aspects about the origin of life are debated. Excluding when or even where it happened, how did life form at all? Most commonly accepted theories are based on experiments in the 1950s that demonstrated organic molecules could be developed from inorganic compounds by simulating the assumed Earth conditions at that time. Yet the evolution of life requires the existence of both genes and proteins, and it is unlikely they would have existed. This presented a significant set of technical problems and the subsequent development of additional theories. To date, we do not know how life evolved on Earth, or even if it originated here. Yet we have an abundance of life on this planet, and the evolutionary journey of life, from whatever origin, is fascinating. Unfortunately, until the fossil record becomes more distinct, the early history of life on Earth is almost as uncertain and debated as the origins of life itself.

The setting in which evolutionary processes began probably consisted of dry bare land and uneroded rocky crust from the pummelling of the Late Heavy Bombardment. As water is essential to the evolution of life, the ancient microbes would have accreted into mats in nutrient-rich waters. The microbial mats were thin layers of diverse microbe species layered on a substrate. This diverse population of creatures with their various survival strategies would, in some cases, find mutually beneficial relationships. The waste products of some species provided nutrients for others, which contributed to supporting the community and its diversity. The mats, when broken up by some form of turbulence, could float away to colonize other favourable areas and increase biodiversity. These mats might have served as the incubators for the free-floating single-celled animals, which form a significant component of the plankton that is so important to the oceans' food chain. Eventually, these microbial mats would be broken up by more complex animals. In the interim, microbial mats were the biological standard, and they remained so for a long time. The next major biological innovation was the development of photosynthesis, estimated to have originated around 3.5 Ga. The original form of photosynthesis was not the oxygenic process we are familiar with today. That form of photosynthesis would not evolve for another billion years (circa 2.5 Ga), and when it did, it would have a staggering impact.

Oxygenic photosynthesis released unprecedented levels of oxygen into Earth's waters and atmosphere. Initially, the oxygen was generally bonded with other common elements, notably sulphur and iron. Over time these oxygen sinks reached their absorptive capacity, and free oxygen accumulated in the waters and atmosphere. However, oxygen, with its fierce capacity to oxidize other elements and compounds, was deadly for many of the extant life forms. This triggered a significant extinction event (circa 2.4 Ga) and opened environmental niches for those organisms that could adapt to the presence of oxygen.

It was a great leap forward for the creatures that adapted to oxygen utilization, because oxygen enabled a faster and more intense metabolism. Sometime after the oxygen extinction event, perhaps as early as 2.2 Ga, the first eukaryote cells began to appear. The origin of the eukaryotes remains uncertain; however, the main theories suggest that at some point the early eukaryotes or proto-eukaryotes were entered by a bacterium, either through ingestion or parasitic attack. If the invader could avoid being digested and did not kill the host, a symbiotic relationship could occur that over time might result in an adaptive success of the two different organisms. As the organisms became more interdependent and gradually shared genetic material, they would move toward becoming a single organism.

At this point, Earth was similar topographically to how we know it today. There was oxygen in the water and the atmosphere, and all three forms of life—eukaryotes along with the earlier archaea and bacteria—existed.

At perhaps around 1.5 Ga, life begins to employ a new adaptive strategy—multicellularity. It is believed that the process of forming multicellular life forms occurred separately many times and with many types of early organisms. There are multiple theories of how this might have occurred. Regardless of how it happened, this new adaptive strategy began an earth-changing event and initiated the evolutionary processes we know today.

A great leap in the movement toward modern biology took place in what has become known as the Cambrian Explosion. This event began about 540 million years ago and lasted between 20 and 25 million years. During this time, there was an accelerated diversification of animal species. These diverse life forms possessed the capacity to occupy unexploited niches within the environment to eventually occupy nearly all of Earth's regions, land, and water. According to modern research, it appears this "explosion" may not have been quite as sudden as once thought; nonetheless, it is of great significance in the diversification of life.

There are three main lines of thought about why this event occurred, the first being environmental changes: increased oxygen, the ozone layer development, and so on. The second line of thought represents developmental arguments, which include complex gene initiation processes and the possibility of horizontal gene transfer. Finally, ecological factors are cited, such as the "arms race" between prey and predator or the rebound effect from a mass extinction that proceeded during this period. There are no conclusive answers. Instead, it appears likely that the answer lies in a combination of several factors.

The next major event in the history of life-form development came about 480 to 444 million years ago as multicellular life began to colonize the land. These early pioneers were simple plants restricted to the shores of the oceans, lakes, and rivers, with minimal impact on the remaining dry land environment. It was not until about 385 to 359 million years ago that complex plant ecosystems covered most of the planet's environmentally suitable land surface.

About 428 million years ago, the earliest known air-breathing land invertebrate, a type of early millipede, appears in fossil records. Most of the early life on land seems to have been composed of arthropods (crustaceans, millipedes, insects, etc.), with scant records of other life forms. This seems reasonable, as arthropods were well adapted to colonize land; their jointed exoskeletons provided protection against desiccation, support against gravity, and a means of locomotion that was not dependent on water. The first evidence of terrestrial snails and flying insects can be dated to the Carboniferous period (358–298 million years ago). By the end of the Carboniferous, many of the common terrestrial invertebrates that we know today were present on land.

Somewhat before the first flying bugs (370–360 million years ago), terrestrial vertebrates challenged the supremacy of the arthropods. It appears tetrapods, four-legged creatures, evolved from a widely distributed ancestor of today's lungfish. Lungfish have one or two lungs and can stay out of the water for periods ranging from a few days to a year. The lungfish larvae have external branched gills, much like newts, and the young also go through a metamorphosis similar to amphibians in order to become mature lungfish. Fossil evidence reveals that a four-legged aquatic air-breathing fish-like creature was the likely transitional life form.

Such entities would continue to develop a more robust skeleton and skin suitable for populating the land; however, unfortunately, a similar transitional version of this creature remains absent from terrestrial fossil records.

The gap in the fossil record ends conclusively around 313 million years ago, with discovered fossils of animals fully capable of living permanently in a dry land environment. These creatures had developed skin that would resist dehydration and eggs with sturdy membranes for survival in a dry environment. Known as amniotes, the creatures evolved and diversified into groups that would become the ancestors of the reptiles, dinosaurs, birds, and mammals, yet generally with reptilian appearance and modest size.

This situation appears to have persisted until about 252 million years ago, when the greatest extinction event ever known occurred. Called the Permian-Triassic Event, this catastrophe brought about the loss of an estimated 90 percent of marine species and 70 percent of terrestrial vertebrates. It is unclear what caused the event, but possible factors include meteorites, climate change, volcanism, and/or changes in the composition of the atmosphere. Whatever the trigger, the result was an extinction of land species that had taken a great deal of time to evolve.

As life slowly rebounded, two groups of vertebrates arose from the archaic amniotes: one that would eventually lead to the development of mammals, and a second that initiated the evolution of dinosaurs, reptiles, and birds. Although beginning as a relatively small and obscure grouping, the second line began to develop as distinct entities from 234 to 232 million years ago and proliferate over the next millions of years, giving rise to the age of the dinosaur. These great beasts would dominate the environment while lesser creatures, the ancestors of mammals, survived in their shadow. This phase of evolution continued until yet another cataclysmic extinction event around 65 million years ago.

The Cretaceous-Paleogene extinction event caused the annihilation of dinosaurs other than the line that had given rise to the first birds. Except for a few species, including sea turtles and crocodiles, no species with an average weight of over 25 kilograms survived. This event has conclusively been shown to have resulted from a massive meteor strike, although some scientists believe there were other contributing factors. One result of this event was yet another biological rebound, where a large, vacated ecological niche became available for exploitation by rapidly multiplying diversified mammals. In addition, surviving birds and smaller reptiles spread both physically and genetically across the landscapes. It had become an age of mammals, to mark the end of the Mesozoic era and the beginning of today's Cenozoic era.

Some vertebrates had lived in the relative safety of forest canopies for millennia, and early mammals followed suit. Some of these tree-dwelling mammals would leave the trees and eventually give rise to the great apes, which in turn ultimately gave rise to the species Homo.

PATTERNS AND CONCLUSIONS

My purpose in providing an overview on the evolution of the cosmos, and of life on Earth, is to set the stage for an examination of the deep patterns that lie beyond the hard evidence. It is at this point that I would like to diverge from a strictly scientific point of view. Scientists tell us of the Big Bang and suggest that evolutionary forces were set from that point forward. Yet the concept of the cosmos's beginning, out of nowhere and from nothing, seems like magical thinking. Although we are bound by space-time, whatever existed before the Big Bang had created space-time and was therefore not bound by it. It is very difficult to conceptualize a beginning that does not exist in a place or time. To date, science has not resolved the serious challenge of understanding the origin of the cosmos. To address this matter, I propose we investigate patterns and determine whether there is a signature in the cosmos that gives a clue to resolving this dilemma.

Order

Some of my earliest memories are of being in nature. I loved nature and was in awe of what I saw and experienced—the power yet delicacy, the profound order among seeming chaos. As I began to study the sciences in school, my curiosity and wonder increased; everything in nature appeared to be underpinned by order. I was taught that all of the amazing phenomena could be explained by natural laws, and some of the wonder was dampened as I bought into the strict scientific paradigm. But after many years of study and contemplation, the rigidity of my scientific views would soften. My journey instilled in me a deep desire to understand the magnificent order that I had recognized and been in awe of as a child.

I began to view the laws of nature differently, not as inaccurate, but rather in terms of their incompleteness. This gave me pause for thought: Could we be missing something critical here? Reductionist thinking has allowed us to take things apart and understand the fundamental physical laws governing them. These laws have proven to be of great practical value. This is perhaps why we tend to look no further at the deeper questions. However, reductionist thinking does not support our looking at how the laws of nature relate quite seamlessly to create a whole, self-sustaining system that appears to be greater than the sum of its parts. Nor does that way of thinking support us to gain an understanding of the how and why of our universe's dynamic perfection.

Dynamic Balance

Not only is the universe specifically ordered, but that order maintains a meticulous balance. On every level, the universe is active yet in balance. Galaxies collide, stars explode, meteors cause mass extinction, civilizations fall, individuals kill and die, and the very cells of our bodies decay. For each of these destructive events, there are constructive countermeasures, and the whole, immensely complex and vast manifestation sustains itself. The tension of centrifugal and gravitational forces maintains our galaxy in its elegant spiral, and the balance of explosive force against gravitational force keeps our Sun from exploding or collapsing. The dynamics of manifestation continue to maintain sustainability, yet are chaotic enough to enable evolution and change.

Lifespans

Dynamic balance and evolution depend on a finite lifespan of manifestation's constituent components. Everything appears to have a lifespan. In fact, it is theorized that every universe has a lifespan. Stars have a lifespan, as do humans and bacteria. Lifespans are nature's way of refreshing herself—a resetting of the elements in the field of manifestation.

Every element of manifestation appears to have a period to achieve its contribution to the manifestation, and then it ends. Stars offer heat and light throughout their lives, while generating heavier elements within themselves by way of their intense nuclear reactions. Upon a star's death, supernovas produce additional heavy elements and throw them into space. This is an essential process in the evolution of Earth-like rocky, mineral-rich planets. Human beings are much the same. Throughout our lives, we have the chance to contribute to the unfolding of manifestation—a child, our creativity, our works. Then we are swept away. The cycle of birth, union, offspring, and death allows evolution to be reasonably rapid and adaptable.

Things Come Apart and Things Unite
In the current context, *solve et coagula* is used to describe a fundamental process that underpins the concepts of birth and death, creation and destruction, simply stated as "things come apart and things unite." This process occurs on the fundamental level of subatomic particles through to the galactic level. It drives all nuclear, chemical, biological, and cosmological processes; it is essentially the most fundamental driving process in the evolution of the cosmos and life.

Gravitation
Gravitation is a natural phenomenon by which masses—objects ranging from atoms and photons to planets and star—are attracted toward one another. Gravity is the weakest of the four fundamental forces of physics that are responsible for shaping the universe we inhabit; the others are electromagnetism and the strong and weak nuclear forces. While the effects of gravity at the subatomic level are negligible, on the macro level it is the most dominant of the forces affecting every physical structure and process, from the formation of galaxies to lunar tides and the shape of the human femur. Gravity is a key feature of the physical universe that appears to have originated within the Big Bang.

Anomalies and Paradoxes
In the study of the evolution of the cosmos, and of life on Earth, it becomes apparent that some rather odd phenomena have enabled their development at critical times.

On the cosmic level, there is the example of the universe's rate of expansion. Had the expansion rate been any slower, the universe would have long since collapsed back onto itself. If the expansion rate had been any faster, the universe would have blown apart and never created the cosmic structures that exist today. The universe's critical rate of expansion perfectly matches its density—a constant set at the instant of the Big Bang. The window that allows a "flat" (stable) universe is very, very narrow, and it is more than a little interesting that it was virtually perfect for the creation of our universe.

While the flat universe is a striking example of an unusual feature of our universe, there are other phenomena, such as the "faint young sun paradox," that are worth noting in relation to the evolution of life on Earth. The energy emitted by our Sun shortly after Earth's formation is calculated as being less than is required to produce liquid surface water. Yet geological records reveal that liquid surface water existed—a contradiction to physical facts, given the heat retention of Earth's atmosphere at the time. Although future explanations may emerge for these dilemmas, their existence is rather amazing. Even more interesting is that life would not have evolved had these mysterious happenings not occurred. Earth retained liquid water (it did not evaporate into space), a critical factor in the evolution of life, despite the "faint sun" and the Late Heavy Bombardment. During the Late Heavy Bombardment, it is postulated Earth was so heavily pummelled by meteorites and comets that almost all of its crust was pulverized into a molten mass. How water was retained on Earth's surface or in its atmosphere remains unknown.

Life itself is perhaps the most amazing mystery and we, to this day, do not know how or in what localized environment it first arose. Nor do we know with certainty when life began. It is conventionally thought to have begun shortly after the Late Heavy Bombardment ended, between 3.7 to 3.5 Ga. However, there is a theory, though a controversial one, that places the origin of life well before the Late Heavy Bombardment to as early as 4.2 Ga. Even if the most conservative figure of 3.5 Ga is correct, life began, in geological terms, very shortly after Earth's formation—a time when Earth had a considerably more hostile environment than today for supporting life as we currently know it.

Other unique features aided Earth's creation and development, including an electromagnetic field that shields us from most of the Sun's solar wind and a large, relatively close moon that creates significant tides. The latter played a role in life's beginning, and it is a critical factor in the transfer of life forms from water bodies to land.

The "fine-tuned universe" is a proposition that evolutionary conditions can only occur when universal fundamental physical constants exist within a very narrow range. Had any of these fundamental constants been slightly different, it is unlikely the universe would be conducive to the establishment and development of matter, astronomical structures, elemental diversity, or life. This proposition has been controversial. Some scientists and philosophers deny it, while others attempt to determine the fine-tuned physical constants' margin of error.

Biophilic Universe

Given the above observation on anomalies and paradoxes, I have come to the conclusion that the universe is biophilic, that it is tuned to the manifestation of physical reality and the evolution of life. We do not know whether other life exists in the universe; however, we have seen that the necessary things happened on Earth to make good on the potential. While I personally believe there is life elsewhere in the universe, I do not think the universe teems with life. And although I believe there is a biophilic bias, life only appears to be possible under certain very favourable conditions.

The ideas that I am putting forward are not an attempt at a scientific theory, but rather a metaphysical conjecture that goes beyond science while remaining compatible with it. The hope in offering these concepts is that it may inspire us to reassess what it is to be human and how, and for what, we are living.

A DIFFERENT PERSPECTIVE

Although the Big Bang is almost certainly the singularity that manifested the universe, I find it difficult to accept the notion that at one instant there was absolutely nothing, and then at the next there was an entire cosmos filled with billions of galaxies. It is counterintuitive; one's mind demands a theory that would lend it believability. Even the development of a theory is a challenge, when we are creatures that evolved and live in a space-time universe. Where does one begin to examine a dimensionless conundrum?

Science's ability to formulate a sequence of events beyond the threshold of space-time creation remains an open question. This is understandable because science, at least the way it is practised in current times, requires empirical evidence before declaring that something exists. Fortunately, for the purposes of speculation, we have access to a tool that science cannot base a theory on—imagination or what some would call rational intuition. I do not mean fantasy, frivolity, or wild daydreams; rather, it involves an open and creative inquiry into possibilities. This is what the old alchemists referred to as true imagining, a particular process to develop and contemplate possibilities. To prime and fuel true imagining, I have looked at the patterns extant in the universe and attempted to reverse-engineer the process.

I believe cosmic love was the initial condition and ground of being that inspired the Big Bang and the creation of the universe. By its nature, as a dimensionless impetus, cosmic love is difficult to comprehend. One might think of it as an intention of infinite creativity—the longing, even the lust for manifestation, for realizing the creative impulse, for experiencing the intensity of an existence. It could be described as the profound ache to experience the ever-deepening knowledge of self that results from the expression of love.

Despite the immense potential and passion to become, cosmic love in its pure state could not realize itself; something more needed to happen. At some undefinable point, cosmic love split itself into two (bifurcated). And at some unknown point, it united again (fusion). This union initiated the Big Bang or what could be thought of as the act of cosmic conception. This sequence was the first example in our comprehensible cosmos of the principle of *solve et coagula*, or separation and joining, a sequence that is a consistent universal operation of manifestation.

All growth and change in manifestation follow this pattern in some fashion. Atoms themselves break up and fuse with dramatic results; the joining and separation of different atoms to form molecules is the backbone of chemistry and biology. Cells split and fuse in the process of reproducing life. The stars come into being from the joining of hydrogen masses, and after eons, ultimately explode into the elements that form the cosmos. Everywhere, on every level, things join for a while and then come apart. It is this self-similarity throughout our known universe that suggests the creation event was of the same ilk, yet on a nearly infinite scale.

This raises the obvious question: How do we conceive of the two things love divides into, and what do we call them? What would be capable of uniting and exploding into all the potentials of a new cosmos? This is a matter currently beyond our ability to see with the eye of empiricism. However, the question is not immune to inquiry through deductive reasoning and contemplation. The point of departure for further exploration is the simple question: What is the cosmos composed of? What we experience as solid matter is a matrix of organized energy. All definable phenomena are composed of organized energy. In reality, there are but two things that form everything in the cosmos: energy and order.

I take this one step further by aligning with ancient thought, rather than the modern mind, to conclude that the ordering principle is consciousness: some immensely elegant and powerful form of awareness and intention sufficient to order the staggering amount of available energy to create a self-sustaining universe.

Consciousness of this magnitude is as difficult for us to understand as cosmic love, given our comparatively limited capacity. However, there is a similarity between cosmic consciousness and human consciousness, just as there is a similarity between cosmic love and human love. We are self-similar to these cosmic forces, or put more simply, we are a chip off the old block. We resemble that from which we arose; however, it is inevitable that when we think in terms of love, energy, and consciousness on the cosmic level, we project onto the cosmic elements our limited, underdeveloped, frightened, and human versions of the concepts. This projection creates yet another class of category error—conceptualizing one level of reality through the perceptive field (or projections) of another. In this case, it is the eye of the human observing the essence of the cosmos. There is a similar struggle for accuracy when we peer into the subatomic level.

Despite the challenges of perceiving clearly, it is possible to recognize the two primal constituents of the cosmos: consciousness and energy. The Big Bang, with its immense creative power, becomes understandable when we imagine it as a nearly infinite amount of energy imbued with a nearly infinite level of consciousness or intention. Through this union, consciousness infused the energy with the capacity for structure in an exceptionally short time, and this in turn created the unimaginably energetic expansion called the Big Bang.

Little wonder that the best metaphor to describe the Big Bang event is an explosion, a unique explosion that has only happened once in our reality—an explosion of creativity. Love bifurcated itself in order to differentiate into components that could creatively interact with each other, recombining to initiate endless, reverberating cycles of splitting and joining, giving rise to a continuous cosmic evolution. I believe the following quote from Andrew Harvey (andrewharvey.net) expresses it beautifully: "Everything is conceived in ecstasy, everything is sustained in ecstasy and everything ends in ecstasy." (In my opinion, the term *love* could easily be substituted for *ecstasy*.)

Propensity Toward Life
But why? Why would a universal singularity like cosmic love feel called upon to become involved with anything, let alone something as fun and exciting as creating the universe? I believe the answer is bound up with why love is the fundamental principle in the first place. It is because only love, of all conceivable forces and principles, is driven inexorably toward life, being, and realization. It appears to revel in increasing complexity, sentience, and an evolving dynamic balance. It is the life force of the cosmos, and its very nature is the longing for expression that compelled it to the great creative act of the Big Bang. A fairly simple way to express this is the paradox of love: It longs to create something more than itself despite the fact that, potentially, love is all there is.

Cosmic love is ineffable, which is why we have difficulty describing it. We view it through the lens of our human projections. We see it "through a glass darkly" (1 Corinthians 13:12) as it is felt in the heart, attempted in our actions, intuited in our spirit, yet nearly inscrutable to the conscious mind. Perhaps this is so because it is a principle that encompasses and is greater than the mind, an order of magnitude beyond our consciousness. The mind knows it is there and that it is real, yet articulating its insights has traditionally been relegated to the work of bards, artists, and mystics. It is so encompassing as to leave us beggared for a simple definition in linear logical terms.

While my intuition about what brought the Big Bang into being cannot be backed with evidence or mathematics, I believe it is consistent with the principles of nature that are extant in our present universe, which I see as the child of the primordial origin. And if my intuition is correct, then there is intention and therefore meaning in the nature of the universe.

Teleology

The term *teleology* has long been in disfavour, if not distain, in scientific and philosophical circles. This is understandable, given the more archaic notions associated with it—of God or gods/goddesses creating the world and the special place of humanity in the universe. Therefore, I would like to make it very clear what I am referring to when using the term *teleology*. I am speaking here not of any creator or intelligent design, nor implying any particular importance to our species or any other life form, carbon-based or otherwise. Rather, I am referring to an implicate order, something as intrinsic to our universe as the cosmological constant or any of the other dimensionless, physical constants. The nature of this implicate order is to produce a universe with the stable but dynamic structures that we see, and to have a slight, but definite, bias toward life.

I am not suggesting that an entity, force, or deity created order within the universe; the universe is simply the way it is, since its first moments. This view is consistent with the assertion that cosmic love, the fundamental ground of being, held an intention to realize itself in the finest possible balance of consciousness and energy, or spirit in matter and matter inspired. Consistent with the intention of a refined self-realization, the bias toward life is not limited to the human expression of life. If we were to drive ourselves to extinction, another branch of life would likely arise to take over as the ruling sentience on this planet. In addition, there is a reasonable probability of other planets with life forms engaged in similar evolutionary processes.

Although the universe's bias toward life is real, it is minimal, just enough to form a stable dynamic to make life possible. The reason for the slightness of the positive bias is that if the predisposition toward life were much greater, the impetus to evolve would be commensurately reduced. It is the challenges of survival, along with relatively short lifespans, mutations, and adaptations to environmental change that drive the evolution of more complex and aware life forms. If life did not face challenges and seek opportunities, we might have remained simple single-celled sea creatures. Our reality is that of adversity, death, and extinction, where responses to the stressors have driven the development of life to ultimately give rise to our species and the beautiful and complex environment in which we live.

An Intelligent Universe
If the universe is made up of the synthesis of energy and consciousness, then it stands to reason that everything is infused with a degree of consciousness and, therefore, carries its own form of sentience. While the term *sentient* is usually reserved for animate creatures with responses and intelligence similar to our own, I believe there is an expression of intelligence in all life forms. Even a simple atom of hydrogen contains, along with its energy, enough information to sustain its stability, unique properties, and ability to govern its interactions. This capacity might seem too primitive to qualify as intelligence; however, it can be argued that a hydrogen atom represents a fundamental unit of intelligence—a building block at its simplest level. With organic chemicals, some very complex molecules form intricate bonds and relationships with other chemicals. From this point, it is a small, yet mysterious, step to life where sentience becomes more obvious. Even the simpler life forms know how to absorb and process nutrients and reproduce. By the time creatures can take on shapes and/or move, they have reached a far more apparent form of sentience—the ability to react directly with

the environment. Plants and fungi will move toward the light or around obstacles, while mobile, single-celled animals will seek food and move toward positive conditions or away from negative environments (levels of light, heat, chemical composition, etc.). These responses become subtler and more complex as life moves to a multicellular level, with the development of specialized nerve cells and sense organs.

The evolutionary process pushed this line of development because it was successful. Nervous systems and brains became ever more complex, leading to life forms that could respond not just to the physical environment but also to their social-emotional, intellectual, and spiritual context. Evolution progressed from the simple intelligence and capacities of the atomic elements to the complex molecules that gave rise to life and, ultimately, our species. This evolutionary progress is founded on the unfolding of an intention inherent in the very nature of the universe, not some kind of cosmic happy accident.

The concepts of teleology and an intelligent universe are often met with intense resistance and criticism. However, in my view, the universe itself presents an overwhelming offering of concrete evidence for the presence of implicate intelligence and intention. There appears to be little evidence of serious scientific inquiry into cosmic intention and intelligence, which sells us short of understanding the true nature of the universe.

There are competing theories on the nature of the universe, and as yet, we have not arrived at any kind of consensus. The proposition of an intentional fine-tuned universe is a good fit with observations and current science. It serves to answer more questions than it raises. The concepts are simple and elegant and grounded in historically verified information. And yet, I cannot know that this proposition is correct; if science cannot yet penetrate back further than the Planck epoch, how could I do so, other than with my imagination?

Chapter Seven

Spirituality

If we accept the idea that the universe arose and is sustained by cosmic love, then what it means to be human is markedly different from what it would be in the mechanistic universe of reductionist theory. I believe this perspective is worth exploring.

THE GREAT QUESTIONS

The question "Is the universe friendly?" or some variant of it has often been attributed to Albert Einstein. Scholars are pretty clear that this is a misattribution, but it remains a good question. I do not believe the universe is friendly, but I do believe it is loving. Although unconcerned with my individual success or failure, biological or otherwise, the universe is predisposed toward the evolution of ever more complex and aware systems. Its structures and natural laws are hospitable to life; the more we align with those, the more likely we are to survive and thrive. The bias is toward viable dynamic systems that evolve and develop in complexity. We have the opportunity, with our human consciousness, to understand and align with the universe. And in that sense, I believe we are loved by the universe.

If the universe is indeed loving and biased toward life, then this has huge ramifications for our species, raising questions of the utmost significance and narrowing the range of appropriate answers to those questions. Such a concept is a clear call to awakening and responsibility.

A universe founded on cosmic love, that has intention embedded in a pervasive implicate order, and therefore a purpose (which I refer to as "the divine purpose"), is far different from the mechanistic "happy accident" universe of reductionism. The implications are huge. All the great questions of existence must be reassessed. What is a human being? If the universe has purpose, then surely, we must have purpose. And what might that be? Are we in some way responsible to something greater than ourselves? If so, how do we align ourselves to this greater purpose? If we are part of a loving universe, what is the nature of "evil"? Why is there so much conflict and suffering in the world?

In light of the absence of personal gods or goddesses, the idea that there may be real meaning in life and that we may be called to be responsible to something other than ourselves would likely yield a different set of answers than were offered by previous eras and perspectives. Similarly, if the concept of evil turns out to be very much a human construct, then we may be called to face our authorship.

What Is Evil?

I do not believe the universe is either good or evil; the concept simply does not apply. The terrifying cataclysms that beset us—earthquakes, violent weather, climate change, volcanic activity—are the products of nature maintaining the amazing dynamic balance that has allowed life on our planet to survive for billions of years. In my time working in the forests on the north coast of British Columbia, Canada, I saw bears stalking does that were about to give birth to their fawns. The bear was not so much after the doe, but after the fawn she was about to drop; baby deer made a good dinner for a bear. Is that cruel or evil? Neither; it is yet another expression of cosmic love. When the bear is successful, it is love of the bear, and when the doe successfully evades the bear, it is love of the deer. In fact, it is good for both species to have this gritty competition for survival, as it supports their evolution. Nature is neither cruel nor evil, just impersonal.

Evil is a human creation. Our construct of evil is an amalgam of ignorance, fear, and maladaptive instinctual responses. Our conception of evil is situational. For example, at one time it was a matter of prestige in Western culture to own slaves, something that is now seen as abominable and unacceptable.

For the purposes of this discussion, I am defining *evil* as that which does harm to the unfolding of evolution at any level. This means harm to self as well as to others, the environment, and our relationship to the mystery of existence. So if we accept that evil exists, and it is a human construct, then this brings up a question of why.

If the fundamental ground of being is love, and we ourselves are part of this divine purpose, then why would we commit harm? Would not a world whose source is cosmic love be perfect, beautiful, and peaceful? Apparently not.

A simple way of describing this paradox is to use the analogy of a prism. Cosmic love expressed on our level can be seen as similar to a beam of pure light being broken down in a prism into its various colours. The clearer and more unflawed the crystal of the prism, and the more perfect and symmetrical the prism, the purer, more beautiful, and truer the output of the many colours it produces. Conversely, the darker and more flawed the prism's crystal, the more the output is flawed and distorted. The key is the quality of the prism; in other words, the quality within us is what filters and then manifests the love. Cosmic love is the starting point—the alchemical *prima materia*—of life, but we do the operations to create gold, or slag, from it.

Opportunism, Oppression, and Violence

Opportunism is an ancient response to the environment; at one time, it was necessary for the individual and their tribe's survival. In those times, resources were often limited but the population was low, so taking what you could get, when you could get it, did little harm to others or the environment. This ancient instinct has survived into our modern day and has become maladaptive. Today it does harm to grab all you can get for you and yours. It has become important to temper our response to not further overtax our environment. It is a matter of finding the balance between our instinctual impulse and our spiritual awareness of connection to Earth and all of life.

Oppression of others is a form of opportunism that is often rooted in economics and anchored in the refusal to see the other as fully human and deserving of inherent respect. This objectification is generally exacerbated and even codified by cultural acceptance, making it harder for an individual to break out of their spiritual darkness and stand against it.

Possibly the ultimate objectification of people is organized warfare. We humans have always had the capacity to fight other human beings for survival. Defending hunting or fishing territory or driving a weaker hunting group off one's kill were likely occasional occurrences in the Paleolithic period. It was not until sometime in the Neolithic period that we started to have the population, accumulated wealth, and motivation to begin to organize specifically for raiding and planned warfare. By the Bronze Age, warfare had become an institution, and it remains so to this day. Why has something so obviously terrible remained so stubbornly a part of human behaviour?

The answer is not simple. It is rooted in an ancient survival instinct, supported by tribalism and dominance. Humans have long seen our species as separated into "my group" and "others," with my group inevitably being better than the others. This supports our ability to objectify the others as inferior, undeserving, and even sub-human, making it far easier to kill and maim. This propensity to tribalism has been shamelessly exploited in conditioning both the civilian and military populations to support war efforts.

Then there is the issue of dominance, the lust to prove that we are indeed superior and deserve to rule over others. There is something almost erotic in the drive to dominate that makes it worth the attempt, even though we risk the possibility of death or defeat.

There is yet another factor that seems to clinch the deal and create a deadly double bind. In *The Parable of the Tribes* (1984) and *Out of Weakness: Healing the Wounds That Drive Us to War* (1988), Andrew Bard Schmookler presents the concept that when one group is attacked by another, there are limited choices of response, all of which lead to militarization. If we surrender when attacked, we face either annihilation or assimilation. Or we can choose to arm ourselves and fight back, thus becoming militant ourselves. Schmookler suggests that thousands of years of this double bind have left us in constant fear of attack and thus in constant preparations for defence. This is the state we find ourselves in to this day.

It is a big step to be aware of maladaptive instinctual responses and curb them to fit within an individuals' spiritual ideals. The fear instilled in us through thousands of years of mutual predation seems to be one of the hallmarks of civilization to date. I do not believe the changes required to address this tendency can be achieved by legislation. With the spiritual growth of enough individuals, the legislation will follow. In short, the challenge of world peace is a personal quest for spiritual awareness.

Aligning with Cosmic Intention

Each of us is a small individual parcel of the cosmic love unfolding through the patterning of the human archetype and the template of carbon-based life on Earth. Humans are a particular form of evolutionary stepping stone, as nature tests our species' viability in response to the cosmic challenge that invites us to play an active part in the unfolding and evolution of life. We have some significance as individuals, yet no greatness. Nature takes a very limited interest in our individual lives. However, we have purpose on the cosmic level: We are part of an evolving species.

In this capacity, each individual can serve through their life experience, informing the human collective and thus shaping and informing the archetypes that will sustain Earth and future generations and will support the betterment of our species in harmony with all others. Finding our individual response to contribute to the evolution of our species lends meaning to our lives. Having meaning guides our direction in an uncertain existence and allows us to gain satisfaction from our endeavours. The absence of meaning plays a large role in depression, an affliction all too common in our era that robs us of joy and our capacity to contribute to life.

Although I believe the universe has intention, I do not see any evidence compelling us to serve that intention. Many have lived long and materially successful lives with no higher objective than their own self-aggrandizement. Given that the universe arose through cosmic love's intention, aligning and providing service within it brings richness and meaning to our lives. As a result, we can experience a profound sense of joy, fulfillment, and authenticity.

When I talk about loving intention, I am referring to the impetus toward being and becoming—the urge toward life that has evoked this living universe. On this level, love is impersonal and impartial, moving toward its own objectives through great dynamic patterns, or laws of nature, that care little for any particular species and less for the individual. Life and the universe is cosmic love becoming.

Human love is a tiny, imperfect holographic splinter of cosmic love. I say imperfect because as creatures that generally perceive themselves as separate, individual, and mortal, we face challenges that the greater universe does not. Fear and attachment interfere with our capacity to align with the field of love that we are embedded in, therefore making it difficult to reach our potential for loving and being loved. This is another aspect of the cosmic challenge as it applies to our lives.

THE SPIRITUAL RESPONSE

Spirituality, as I define it, is our understanding of and relationship to the great questions of life. There is a deep history of spiritual expression in our species' evolution. From early humans to the present day, we have been responding to a spiritual intuition: the felt sense that something of us transcends death, that there is something going on that is greater than ourselves, and that we can be in relationship with that something. From deep antiquity, we have made special efforts to bury our dead. Ancient paintings and carvings imply an attempt to be in relationship with the broader flow of life. Since the end of the Paleolithic period, we have been building and decorating special places of communion with spirit, in some form or other; this activity continues to this day across most cultures.

Traditionally, as with all aspects of life in the deep past, the response to the impetus of spiritual intuition was set in a tribal context. As we passed through the transformation of the Neolithic into the Bronze Age, the social context grew, first to the village, then to the city-state, and later to the nation. An ancient city-state, nation, or civilization gained numerous benefits from social cohesion and identity. These characteristics supported stability and gave the capacity to merge tribes, which resulted in an economy of scale for everything from architecture to agriculture and war. Religion made the nation strong, and the nation established religion as a normal and long-term social structure. It was one answer to the impetus of the spiritual intuition and was well suited to illiterate cultures. Conformity was enforced, and the comforts of certainty would have supported the people to conform. Hence, for a long time in our history, religion of various kinds has been the standard response to the spiritual inclination.

With the birth of philosophy, people began to look at the world and its phenomena from a different perspective, seeking answers from reason and observation rather than from strictly mythic and mystical perspectives. While most philosophers appeared to respect the deities of their culture, certain questions in life seemed to be better answered outside of religion, thus opening a schism between religion and philosophy. This schism continued into late antiquity, when the Western civilizations underwent two critical shifts in trajectory.

First, the mighty Roman Empire embraced the relatively new Christian religion. Not long afterward, the Western Empire collapsed under the invasions of so-called barbarian tribes. These barbarians were illiterate people who disrupted the social institutions of the Roman Empire in the areas they conquered. However, the Christians held a monopoly on education and learning, and they began to diligently convert the barbarians. Philosophy was considered within a Christian context, closing the gap between philosophy and religion.

Toward the end of the 13th century CE, things began to shift with the appearance of the first universities. With the rise of the Renaissance in the 14th century through to the Age of Enlightenment in the 17th century, several momentous cultural shifts took place.

The work of Gutenberg in the mid-1400s sparked the printing revolution, making ideas and learning available to greater and greater numbers of people. More independent universities were founded, liberating education from the control of the church. The humanist movement of the Renaissance put human beings back into a more primary position in the scheme of things, lifting them above the place of mere servants of God. In the early 16th century, there was unrest within the Christian church concerning its corruption, worldliness, and decadence. This dispute came to a head with the proclamations of Martin Luther, which ultimately boiled over into the Reformation movement.

The result was a return to scriptural literalism and a defence, both ideological and militarily, of the Christian faith. Amid this religious conflict, another force began to assert its early influence: Modern science had begun to emerge. The publication of Copernicus's work on the heliocentric solar system conflicted with the literalism of the Christian faith, and consequently sparks flew. Innovative scientists, notably Galileo, were arrested and charged with heresy. Yet another schism in Western society was beginning, one which would grow in intensity and antipathy in the years to come.

By the Age of Enlightenment in the 18th century, keen intellectual minds were questioning the authority of both the Christian church and the monarchy. The spread of literacy and education gave rise to debate as well as bloody revolutions. Polarization deepened between the church, on the one hand, and philosophical and scientific intellectuals, on the other. Scientific and philosophical thought began to develop its own kind of literalism by assuming that all facets of the human experience could be explained by reason and empirical evidence alone.

In the 19th century, both science and industry surged ahead, the one supporting the other in a dynamic interdependence. People left the land, or were forced off it, to come to the industrialized cities, and the first steps toward universal public education began. Books for both entertainment and education became prevalent; one book of science became immensely important: Charles Darwin's *On the Origin of Species* (1859). This one book had a profound effect on the intellectual community and, later, on the public—an effect so dramatic that it echoes down to the present day. It took the debate between church and science from an intellectual contest to a public war of words. In the following century, highly publicized trials in the United States regarding the appropriateness of teaching evolution or creationism in schools further polarized public opinion. Both sides became entrenched and more aggressive in their doctrines. In 1966, the newsmagazine *Time* carried on its front cover the headline for a lead story titled: "Is God Dead?" The question was a reference to Friedrich Nietzsche's famous quote, "God is dead," published in 1882. The striking magazine cover and the impact of the question shocked the world and no doubt contributed to the social foment of the turbulent 1960s.

Through the 19th and 20th centuries and up to the present moment, science and technology have been making our lives better in countless ways, giving strong messages of reliability and accuracy. This has added weight to the argument of the atheists, while the religious folk dig in and refuse to give up their response to the spiritual impulse. Tribalism and polarization have created a dynamic of "You are either with us or against us," inspiring a social schism that often results in conflict.

Despite all the rhetoric about reason and empiricism and the efforts to debunk religion in our present time, most of the world's population still claims to have some kind of spiritual practice. We have a felt sense of being part of something bigger that lends meaning and purpose to our lives. This response has been dismissed by some as a neurotic need for succour in the face of a meaningless universe.

In our modern times, the grip of religion has slipped and given rise to alternative spiritual responses. One is atheism. The absolute certainty that there is no divine presence in the universe is not only a spiritual standpoint, but also an act of faith. Science points out huge gaps in religious beliefs, but it does not prove atheism is true. Atheism is a belief, like any other unproven belief.

Another alternative spiritual response is what I call the way of the seeker: people searching for answers to the great questions outside the mainstream polarity. In its best form, I believe seeking involves an open-minded inquiry into the mysteries of life, developing a stable but mutable worldview ever open to further information, which may or may not include belief in a divinity of some kind. Other goals might be considered spiritual objectives, such as the development of self-awareness, contribution to a culture that values equality, cooperation, and protection of the environment.

The true seeker accepts that there is no certain knowledge and that most spiritual paths can offer some piece of the puzzle. The most workable beliefs are those that answer more questions than they raise. This perspective creates an openness and flexibility of mind, grasps paradox, and can accept the uncertainty and mutability of life. This is the spiritual path of the individual who wishes to seek their own answers outside of the orthodoxy of either religion or atheism.

The seeker faces a unique and complex issue when it comes to support and guidance. The religious have their clergy, scripture, and God/gods, while the atheist has science and accepted conventional knowledge. Seekers, on the other hand, are on their own with a sea of possibilities. In addition, there is a broad range of credibility and motivation within the vast range of wisdom traditions, teachers, and communities. Thus the seeker needs to exercise discernment in their path to greater consciousness.

The Successful Spiritual Life

Ideally, our spiritual path, whatever it may be, should bring us into a positive, stable relationship with self, other, nature, and the divine. One of the primary projects we need to engage in is to manage our fear and the neurosis that our fear energizes. In a creature as intelligent, sensitive, and aware as a human being, the knowledge of our inevitable death or non-being calls forth a vast spectrum of derivative fears and anxieties. By calming our fear, we are in a better position to make an honest assessment of our neurotic reactions and become open to compassion for self and others. When the heart is opened and the mind is cleared of these reactions, the path to compassion, peace, and universal tolerance becomes possible.

Fundamentalism and literalism are antithetical to spiritual fulfillment. These tendencies can be present in religion, atheism, or the seeker. Within religion, there are ample instances of the fundamentalist viewpoint, where literal interpretation of ancient scriptures advocates strict adherence despite flying in the face of science or reason. The resolute assertion of the atheist, that no form of divine entity or force exists in the universe, cannot be proven; it is a closed-minded form of fundamentalism. Seekers can fall into the same trap of thinking, despite lack of proof, that they have found the one true path. Much blood has been shed due to stubborn fundamentalism.

Humans long for certainty, as it brings a sense of security over the primal fears of existence. But there is no absolute knowing. Questioning assumptions and accepting paradox and uncertainty support the pursuit of a successful spiritual life.

There are many spiritual practices available to us in our current times that can support us to connect more deeply with ourselves, others, nature, and the divine. Ultimately the expression of our spirituality is in how we live our lives. The degree to which we can align ourselves with divine purpose determines our spiritual success.

HUMAN DEVELOPMENT

As far as we know, we are the only beings on Earth with sufficient self-awareness to have required evolution to split consciousness, leaving self-aware consciousness on one side of the divide and the unconscious on the other. While this separation was necessary for humans to evolve thus far, we now have a disconnect from an understanding of our more primal nature. There are many theories about how this split has impacted our development. The theory presented here relies heavily on the work of Carl Jung, Alexander Lowen, and Abraham Maslow.

The development of a human being from conception to delivery can be seen as miraculous on various levels, but for our purposes, I am going to restrict myself to the spiritual aspects. The point at which the building blocks of consciousness are sufficiently constellated to support the development of the primal psycho-spiritual structures is debatable. However, I believe spirituality is a pre-existent condition, and its flowering is tied to the development of the nervous system.

At some point the unborn child becomes aware of sound, movement, and tensions in the mother's body. As development progresses, one theory of human development proposes that the fetus begins to have an unconscious awareness of the myriad of archetypes that are available within the human collective. This is the period when the database of potential archetypes is developed; the process will go on until the dawning of a conscious mind begins to eclipse the unconscious processes. These impressions are not carried consciously into adult life, yet they remain in the unconscious.

During the process of birth and in the following months, there is a massive burst of new experiences and information. This time of life probably represents the most rapid and unbiased collection of data that we will acquire throughout our lives. Although free from personal ego, the data is not free from the constraints of the infant's environment. Infants begin to grasp what works for the achievement of personal benefits and ensuring safety and continuance. The groundwork of character building has begun. Although it will continue for our entire lives, much of what will endure through our lifetime is subconsciously established during this stage.

Through the formative years, the child unconsciously tests and selects various archetypes to embody successful coping strategies. For example, in my family of origin, a boy had to be honest, hard-working, and tough. There was no room for sissy behaviours or soft emotions; vulnerability was a liability. Hence, we pull from the imprinted subconscious data the range of archetypes that seem to work in our world. As these chosen archetypes prove to be apparently successful, we identify with them and shadow the rest. Because this process is unconscious and happens early in life, we fix upon these specific archetypes and lock them into our unconscious. This has a significant impact on our life journey, conception of ourselves, and spiritual development.

If you grew up, as I did, believing you had to be tough because all of life was a struggle and a fight, then guess what? It will be. Our personal mythologies begin to create self-affirming experiences that reinforce those mythologies. If you look for a struggle and a fight, you will indeed find one. Interestingly, not only does our selection of archetypes influence our attitudes and experiences, but it also influences the very structure of our bodies. Habitual ways that we unconsciously direct our body energies, or what I call "charge," cause us to hold or dissipate muscular tensions in various areas of the body. Subtly, over time, our body is shaped by this habituation. Thus, a character structure is formed that visually and energetically tells the rest of the world much about how we operate (see The *Language of the Body* by Alexander Lowen, originally published in 1958). This is something most people lack conscious awareness of, as it takes place below the radar. We read each other even if we are not consciously aware of it. This, too, shapes our experiences. If you look like a fighter, you get a very different response from the world than if you look like a lover. Again, this reaction reinforces the appropriateness of the archetype and the personal mythology, eventually locking us into both. Even if we have awareness in later life that perhaps our archetypes and mythologies are less than successful, it is hard to shift them.

The result is that the formative years shape our attitudes, emotional responses, self-image, or personal mythology and the subtle expressions of our physical bodies. These elements will shape our responses and ideas about the great questions of life, thereby affecting our spiritual experiences and expressions.

We do not change our fundamental archetypes, but we can explore and adjust their expression. Understanding our personal archetypal patterns enables us to make adjustments. Archetypes and character structures have successful and unsuccessful manifestations; the challenge is to sort out which is which and give focus and energy to the desired aspect. Although we do not change our fundamental archetypal nature, we can tune its expression to suit our authentic spiritual goals.

We need a set of beliefs that offers structure and meaning to our being. Healthy, high-functioning humans serve something greater than their own self-interest. As well as a thoughtful and credible belief system, we also need to be aware of the high importance of our relationships to self, others, nature, and spirit (the universe or the divine).

As we are within, so we will be without. The way we relate to ourselves will dictate the manner in which we relate to others, nature, and spirit. The key lies in authenticity—understanding our drives and motivations, tempering that knowledge with gentle, respectful self-compassion, and choosing to live a life where the internal thoughts, feelings, beliefs, and values are congruent with external expression.

Relationships

When we look at relationships to self, others, nature, and the universe or divine, it is important to consider two main questions: What is important about tending to these relationships? And what are our objectives in these relationships? The relationship to self should be seen as absolutely fundamental to the development of the other relationships.

As a social animal, there are many reasons for wanting to relate to another, but how do interpersonal relationships fit into the big picture of life? In addressing this question, it is important to consider that the underlying essence of the universe is cosmic love and that this love seems to be most concisely described as the impetus toward life and its development. Therefore, beliefs and actions supporting the thrust toward life will bring us into a resonance with cosmic love.

Relatively few people have a sound and compassionate knowledge of their own needs, fears, projections, longings, triggers, or other unconscious feelings that motivate their behaviour. To "know thyself" is the key. This is not a quick or easy process, in part because we often quite innocently deceive ourselves about our own nature in order to fit within our desired self-image and to avoid meeting our fears head-on.

If we want harmonious, creative, and loving relationships, then we must understand what we bring to them. If we are seeking to attune ourselves to the universe, self-knowledge is essential to such an alignment.

Critical to the pursuit of self-knowledge is self-compassion. While we dig into our inner processes with forthright honesty, we must also hold ourselves in compassion, because we are likely to discover habits of behaviour that do not serve us in life.

The demon of self-hate is a particularly common by-product of the socialization process, usually developing so insidiously at such a young age that we are scarcely aware of it. The expression of self-hate varies greatly and can, at times, look like successful behaviours from the outside while remaining internally corrosive. Understanding why self-hating behaviours are a part of our lives, and finding ways to moderate them, is an important part of the spiritual work of maturation.

If the pursuit of the relationship to self is tricky, how much more complicated is it when we are in relationships with others? We did not evolve as independent creatures, and even if we could master independence, it would be negating the very thing that allowed our species' survival and success: communication, creativity, collaboration, and compassion. All of these aspects only work in a relational situation. In practical terms, life is about relationships.

In application, the spiritual objectives at the level of relationship to others are numerous and varied, yet they are based on some rather simple principles. We need to consider how we can bring out the best in each other in a way that serves us as individuals, the community at large, nature, and the divine or that which is greater than us. Supporting others to achieve their greatest offering to life, while being respectful of our own needs, can enrich the individual, the other, and society as a whole. While being of service is good for all concerned, in order to be sustainable, there needs to be a depth of satisfaction for the individual on the levels of spirit, mind, or heart that is energetically comparable to the output. If we fail to "balance the energetic books," then eventually we are looking at burnout and collapse, which is good for no one.

Looking at service in this light, there is a pattern that runs through the universe and is reflected in the microcosm of our lives. The analogy I use is that of resonance, where the natural vibration of one object, like a tuning fork, can excite the same vibration in another object. We are derived from the living universe; there is a self-similar natural vibration between the universe and ourselves. As life (the universe) plays on us, it can excite either a dissonance or a resonance response in us, depending on how we tune ourselves. To move toward harmony with the universe is to create a resonance that is in alignment with cosmic love.

The relationship to nature is also very important, as we, too, are animals. For at least the first 200,000 years, our species lived as hunter-gatherers in the natural environment. For only a fraction of that time, at most 10,000 years, we have created artificial environments to live in. For the good of both the natural environment and ourselves, it is essential that we keep contact with our animal nature and the natural environment. Separation from nature has underpinned both the environmental crisis and the dramatic incidence of ennui and depression in our population.

Nature is a picture window into the workings of the divine or cosmic love. Studying a single tree can yield insights into the nature of all life, including our own. The deeper our understanding and emotional connection to the natural world, the more likely we will want to live in harmony with it and curtail the excesses of materialism. We may think we are largely independent of nature, but nothing could be further from reality.

Even before the arrival of modern humans, our genus has been called to grapple with the question of our relationship to the cosmos. We are without doubt spiritual beings. An understanding of the universe seems necessary for humans to make sense of life and to navigate it. Whatever our response, whether it is materialistic atheism, devout orthodox religion, or an independent spiritual path, we are all responding in one way or another to the spiritual drive. It is unavoidably important. The most apparent objective of our relationship to the cosmos is to find our place in it, a psycho-spiritual location from which we can operate.

Taking Stock

Regardless of how we configure our spiritual pursuits, how can we satisfy ourselves that we are getting where we have hoped to go? Given that there is no recognized endpoint to the spiritual journey, we need to be content with taking the measure of the quality of the journey, both within and without. Looking within, one might ask: Am I at peace? Do I feel loved? Can I give love? Am I satisfied with my life? Does life have wonder for me or joy? Changing lenses and looking at one's world, it might be worth asking: Am I loved or regarded? Can I freely offer my creativity? Does the world and its people look beautiful to me? I believe these kinds of questions can be used to "take a temperature" on our spiritual life. Personally, I often use the question: Are the people around me beautiful? If they do not appear so, I know that I have an issue I must address.

Ideally, our spiritual work throughout our lives will help us face life's challenges, find peace in ourselves, family, community, and the greater world, and allow us to bring our greatest creative gifts to the world. If we can do this while maintaining a sense of self-regard and compassion, it could probably be said that we have successfully navigated the challenge of living the spiritual life.

Death

We know we will die. We observe other people, plants, and animals dying and physically dissolving before our eyes. We assume that everything living will die. Even stars die, and physicists tell us that ultimately the universe itself will die. Knowledge that everything, including us, will die, coupled with our type of self-awareness and ego structure, causes ongoing existential stress. Unless managed consciously and with compassion, our attempts to deal with, or avoid, this primal fear of death can cause many and varied dysfunctions and unsuccessful behaviours. Fear of death is a natural consequence of the process of evolution that was built into the nature of animals long before anything that vaguely resembled an ape ever came into being. By the time humans arrived on the scene, a profound survival instinct had developed, and with it, the fear of death. On top of this instinctive response was layered the ever-increasing self-awareness of our species.

Death is essential to the evolution and maintenance of the dynamic balance of life. It plays a role in the ecology and success of a species, as well as its role and effect on the environment. Thus, it would serve us to accept not just the inevitability of death, but also its appropriateness. Bear in mind that evolution is all about life evolving and not so much about the individual's existence.

While the intellectual knowledge that death and the fear of death are natural and appropriate may help with our acceptance of it, there are other ways we can look at it to support a more positive relationship. Cultivating a sense of belonging to the greater unfolding of life and seeing our place in it supports us to see there is something profound going on that all of us, great or small, are playing a part in. For any one human being, that part is limited, but the great unfolding of human potential could not happen without the individual. In a small way, we all carry significance in our life and our death. We need to embrace our significance, see ourselves as players in the cosmic challenge, and know that our eventual passing will not negate any of this.

Perhaps the important thing is to discover the role our authentic personal contribution plays in the cosmic challenge and play that role with passion. This is what Ernest Becker (known for his 1973 book *The Denial of Death*) referred to as the immortality project—the idea that we build a symbolic meaning for ourselves that survives physical death. While I agree with this theory, I do not think that seeking to serve the species by trying to leave it better than we found it is merely about fending off our fear of death.

It also ties into our embracing the cosmic challenge of service to the larger collective and the evolution of our species.

When the chosen pursuit ignites our passion and we live life fully, intensely, and authentically, it is bound to take some of the sting out of the idea of leaving it. The more timid we are in embracing life, the more frightened we are of both life and its ultimate end. The more our passions and dreams are unrealized, the more likely it is that we will feel despair at the prospect of one day losing the chance to express them.

What, if anything, is the fate of a human being after death? One of our fundamental characteristics is of being a temporary aggregation of energies forming the physical self, with a consciousness that directs the physical self's energies. Obviously, the body does not survive death intact, but many theories and beliefs suggest that some aspect of us does survive to exist in another place or plane or experience some kind of rebirth.

My belief is that there is no "returning" to the divine, in life or after death, because we have never left; divinity is as much a part of us as of everything else in the cosmos—it is our nature. If this theory is accurate, then we are pulsations of the divine as it develops toward the ultimate challenge of perfecting spirit in matter and matter inspired. As such, how important is the winking out at the end of our time, as opposed to the extent that we contribute in the time we have? One of the great spiritual milestones for our species in the coming years may be to consciously hold the paradox of being individual while also being part of a larger collective and of being significant without being self-important.

Spiritual Alchemy

I believe that within us, we have the potential to carry out the operations of what I call "spiritual alchemy," the capacity to transmute our ignorance, anger, suffering, and fears into that which is nourishing and beneficial for self and others. By aligning ourselves with the great universal intention on every level—within ourselves, with others, with nature, and with the divine as we perceive it—we can find peace and harmony in all our relationships and contribute to a loving, creative, and sustainable future.

The universe is a self-correcting dynamic system that allows for evolution and growth without sliding into devolution and collapse. Since we are a sub-system of the universe, the alchemical maxim "as above, so below" implies that we, like all life, are self-correcting systems. To access the benefits of our self-correcting nature and utilize the dynamic relationship between ourselves and the environment to the best advantage, we must understand the processes of the body, heart, and mind.

Similarly, the principle "as within, so without" is consistent throughout the universe. For example, characteristics of our Sun—its size, gravitational field, and the amount of energy it releases—have shaped the environment of our solar system. In turn the characteristics of Earth have shaped the environment of our biosphere. Finally we humans have become powerful enough that our inner nature is shaping the environment we live in. It is of extreme importance at this time in Earth's evolution, and our own, that we understand and accept that our modes of thinking and responding are having a huge impact not only on our own lives, but on all life on Earth.

I believe this is a call to responsibility, to consciously develop so that we are more in harmony with ourselves, each other, nature, and ultimately the divine purpose. This brings forth an attendant freedom and power. If we can understand how we create the environment, and therefore the life we have made for ourselves, we have the chance to shape and enhance both.

The essence of spiritual alchemy is a transmutation of life experience to create the "gold" of conscious evolution. The process is analogous to traditional alchemy in that it can be seen in its simplest terms as dissolving, separating, and then coagulating the *prima materia* of experience.

The first function of dissolving (or burning away, known as calcination) is the removal of the dross of the experience. I am using "dross" here to denote the negative residue left by the challenging and painful experiences of life; it can be thoughts, emotions, and/or trauma. It is also significantly affected by our personal makeup and background, including our archetypal structure, our coping strategies, and the beliefs we have acquired from family, religion, culture, and personal experience. The process of dissolving the dross is not one of casting it aside and merely trying to push the painful experience away. It is rather a process of dross purification, so we can proceed with the transmutation work. The idea is to mitigate the sting of the painful incident so we can more clearly see and understand the experience.

In the second phase, we are seeking to separate such things as the real from the imagined, the facts from the interpretations, the responsibility from the blame, and our projection onto others from our shadow.

The third and final stage of coagulation requires discernment and compassionate objectivity—incorporating a deeper learning and bringing it to consciousness, giving new meaning to the experience and providing greater self-knowledge. Through the passion that arises from the mitigated pain, we can separate and define the elements of experience and apply intelligence and tender compassion to yield a new wisdom and peace. Thus we have used the fire of pain to purify the experience.

Cosmic Love

Every class of thing in the universe, including the universe itself, has a signature way of being—an implicate order as well as an explicate form. Rather than trying to unravel the deep complexities of the nature of the universe, it is simpler to look at what the universe appears to be and what it appears to be doing. The existence of our majestic universe is, in itself, amazing. Even more astonishing is the existence of a few dimensionless, finely tuned physical constants without which the universe could not have evolved. This is what I describe as the outward expression in the implicate order of cosmic love. The universe is in a stunning dynamic balance, wherein vast amounts of energy and matter are stable enough to exist over a suitable length of time while remaining mutable enough to allow for expansion and evolution. All these factors point toward another of the universe's profound characteristics. It is biophilic—it has a love of life and supports its evolution.

Earth beautifully exemplifies this characteristic. The fossil record and current biology reveal how life promotes evolution through fostering diversity yet maintaining balance. Furthermore, the evolution of life progressively moves toward increased complexity, self-awareness, and intelligence. There is a pattern of similarity on different scales. What the universe is achieving on a grand cosmic scale, it is also accomplishing in a humbler fashion on a planetary scale, with the evolution of life. It is evolving different structures with similar patterns—a self-similarity revealing one overarching intention of expansion and evolution, supporting life.

If the nature of the universe can be inferred from what it is and what it does, then we have clear guidance with which we can align ourselves for the best possible microcosm of the great macrocosm. The first obvious objective would be to align ourselves with this overarching intention, as much as our understanding and circumstances will allow. This direction would be realized by loving expression in all of the great relationships: to self, others, nature, and spirit as we understand it. If the universe loves life in general—as is evident through its amazing and endless creativity, while pushing life toward greater awareness and sophistication—we should consider doing the same in ourselves and our societies.

The universe favours life and evolution, yet it is not committed to our species. The choice of whether to align with cosmic love is ours to make, as individuals and as a species. I believe our success rests on this decision.

Chapter Eight

Evolution of Our Future

The first ancient efforts to explain the nature of reality did so through mythology. But, perhaps stimulated by the Bronze Age collapse and a rebirth of civilization in Greece, inquiry about the world took a radical turn. By the 7th century BCE, observation, logic, and hypotheses were used to explain natural objects and phenomena. These tools freed human thought from the rigidity of dogma and tradition and opened the field to reason and curiosity. The birth of philosophy was the first step toward science, which initiated a conflict with spiritual intuition that echoes down to this day. Each of us must now construct a belief system that takes into account the unquestionable power of science as well as our spiritual impulses, because we need a stable belief system in order to function effectively.

Our belief systems inform our lives—from how we express ourselves to the kinds of food we find acceptable to eat. They are the source of our motivation and they govern our life paths and behaviours. The construction of these belief systems is based on our intuitive felt sense of spirituality, our rational desire for understanding, programming from our social and cultural environment, our archetypes and our personal mythology, all fused together with an overarching rationalization that can be described as a personal philosophy. This outlook becomes the template for how we perceive, interpret, and live our lives. Personal philosophies taken together meld to form a collective group philosophy, whereby the members of the group share beliefs about family, religion, politics, and so on.

PHILOSOPHY OF THE NEW ALCHEMY

The intention of the new alchemy is to foster a worldview consistent with the observed natural world. It does not contradict scientific knowledge or observed natural phenomena. However, it extends beyond what is generally accepted by science and offers a counterperspective to the dismal reductionist philosophy that says there can be no purpose to the universe.

While science may end up offering an understanding of nature, the question remains how such elegant laws of nature came to be and how it is that we have a finely tuned dynamic universe that has sustained itself for billions of years. The fact that there are consistent laws and principles is not surprising. The mystery is, how did this happen? The "happy accident" model of the universe is not sufficient to explain it. The new alchemy goes beyond scientific fact and looks for a greater unifying principle. Although science suggests that there are no absolute facts and that we know nothing with absolute certainty, the scientific process explores reality and looks for reasonable certainties. The new alchemy seeks to thoughtfully move beyond the accepted facts yet remain solidly consistent with them.

Today, anything that goes beyond reasonably proven science is conjecture. The choices of how to view the world are fairly basic. We can choose to accept science as the sole arbitrator of reality, leaving the many unanswered questions hanging, or we can look for a philosophy that offers tentative solutions to some of the great unanswered questions. It comes down to choice. What kind of philosophy answers more questions than it raises and best serves my ability to live and flourish?

The fundamental aim of the new alchemy is to foster a shift in consciousness that will prepare and support humankind to move through the next great evolutionary bottleneck toward a loving, creative, and sustainable state in the future. To this end, there are general principles that underlie all the concepts.

- **Universality:** We, and everything else in the universe, arose from one source. We are of one thing. In objective reality, it does not matter if the object is a star, a cockroach, or a human being—all are part of the great dynamic unfolding. This fact invites all thinking people to consider and treat every aspect of nature with respect and consideration. That does not mean we should not use the fruits of nature; in fact, we must do so to survive. However, it is not our divine right to take anything and everything we can get. Universality calls us to feelings of respect, mutuality, and humility.

- **Intentionality:** The one great thing from which we all arose, and which we are a dynamic part of, appears to have intentionality woven into its very fabric. This intentionality is part of the implicate order that gives all elements of the universe their particular nature, overall structure, and character. The universe is evolving in a particular direction in order to maintain this order. No one knows this direction or intention, yet a reasonable hypothesis would be that nature is striving for the perfect balance of spirit in matter and matter inspired. If the universe is intentional, then that raises a serious question of responsibility. Are we, as conscious elements of the universe, called to align with the vast intention and take some responsibility? Is there a role for us in the unfolding?

I believe it is incumbent upon us to use our energy, skills, and creativity to align with the universe and attempt to refine the evolving expression of conscious matter.

- **Evolution:** A fundamental assumption of the new alchemy is a commitment to the evolution of the individual, humankind, and our relationship with the greater environment and the divine. The key to evolution is the individual's personal development. We can only create the world we long for externally if we can create the building blocks of it within ourselves. Self-awareness, self-responsibility, and compassion allow us to build, as M. Scott Peck put it, "a world waiting to be born." To have the self-mastery that will allow us to participate in such creativity requires that we understand and are prepared to amend our personal philosophies as our consciousness evolves.

PERSONAL PHILOSOPHY

If we are to investigate our personal philosophy, the place to start is with the simplest of questions: Is it working for me? Am I happy and satisfied in my life? Am I at peace within and without? Do I have a healthy respect for myself? Do I have passion and purpose in my life?

A less subjective indicator of how our philosophy is impacting our life is in our relationships with others. They provide the mirroring, reflecting back how we are seen in the world.

Our relationship to the great questions of life, our spirituality, is an important indication of our personal philosophy. Some choose atheism, while many choose religion, and others select the path of the seeker. It does not matter which choice we make. What matters is that we are seeking and finding meaningful answers while bearing in mind there is no certainty. I believe such seeking is a natural impulse. And even if it seems that our personal philosophy works well for us, it is worth consistently reviewing our inner assumptions, attitudes, and beliefs in order to see more clearly how our worldview impacts our experience and the world we live in.

Reviewing our belief system requires us to cultivate skills of self-exploration and self-awareness. This internal work is iterative. As we learn about ourselves, we are in a better position to understand and more astutely inquire into our beliefs.

One of the first and most critical steps in any process of self-awareness is to cultivate what is called a "witness self." This is an aspect of self that can stand outside our everyday persona and observe what we are doing, thinking, or feeling. It is the act of raising an aspect of mind above the situation in order to see one's own part in that situation. This is not the voice of self-criticism. The witness self does not judge; it merely brings us to a state of consciousness and self-awareness. It is like a subprogram of the mind that asks questions such as: What am I doing right now? Why am I interpreting the situation this way? What is my motivation? What is my projection? This self-witnessing can be applied to any of the four aspects: body, heart, mind, or spirit.

While it is valuable for the witness self to maintain a dispassionate, objective perspective, it is important to maintain a tone of self-compassion in our inquiry. When we come across the inevitable foibles, biases, and inconsistencies that may be disturbing to us, it is worth remembering that our hearts can serve to transmute pain, shame, and despair into energy, passion, and creativity. This work will ultimately free us to live a more authentic and joyful life.

MATURITY

The dictionary definition of *maturity* is broad due to the many ways the term can be applied in the English language. In this context, maturity refers to the degree of an individual's psycho-emotional and spiritual development. This state may not have any correlation to age, as many people experience an arresting of this kind of development at a much earlier age than their chronological age. There is no fixed scale with which to measure maturity. However, the following provides a list of the most significant markers.

- **Self-responsibility:** Holding yourself accountable for the life you have and the way you live it; accepting the authorship of all words and actions or lack thereof. Accepting that we are the creators of our lives and that outside forces, people, circumstances, government, and God are not responsible for the situations in which we find ourselves. We are habituated in our culture to look for whom to blame when something we do not like happens. This is a sign that our development and emotional maturity have been arrested at the simple right/wrong level, which is an abdication of self-responsibility.

    Invictus
    by William Ernest Henley (1920)

    Out of the night that covers me,
      Black as the pit from pole to pole,
    I thank whatever gods may be
      For my unconquerable soul.

    In the fell clutch of circumstance
      I have not winced nor cried aloud.

Under the bludgeonings of chance
  My head is bloody, but unbowed.

Beyond this place of wrath and tears
  Looms but the Horror of the shade,
And yet the menace of the years
  Finds and shall find me unafraid.

It matters not how strait the gate,
  How charged with punishments the scroll,
I am the master of my fate,
  I am the captain of my soul.

- **Self-awareness:** Understanding and accepting the non-material elements of ourselves—which can include our archetypes, character structure, needs, compensations, biases, emotional triggers, desires, and so on—is a life-long endeavour that supports us to attain mastery and make our best contribution to the world.

- **Integrity:** Walking one's talk, fulfilling one's commitments, and living one's life in an open, honest way are some of the ways a person of integrity reveals themselves. Simply put, the idea is to be consistent with our own beliefs and principles in all aspects of our lives.

- **Caring:** An expression of our love and sensitivity to ourselves, others, and the natural world. If we are not taking care of ourselves in all aspects, then we are not doing "job number one" and are likely to end up being part of the problem rather than part of the solution. Our understanding and expressions of love change as we mature. The child's love for their caretaker is seated in dependence, the adolescent's love is caught in the midst of the struggle for individuation, while the more mature love of later life ideally includes a more universal aspect that develops our caring for others, both human and non-human.

There is also the caring about, and for, nature. Our species continues to put a crushing, destructive burden on the environment. There remains a tendency to see the natural world as a great warehouse of resources from which we are entitled to take as much as we want. Humans are naturally opportunistic and have always taken what they needed from the environment. However, we are now called to open our hearts and our minds to the realization that we must override our ancient predisposition if we are to save ourselves and much of the biosphere from extinction.

- **Empathy:** The degree to which one can sense another's suffering and feel compassion for them is an important signifier of maturity. Narcissism, on the other hand, is the degree to which a person expects the interest, support, and focus of others. The two aspects can be viewed as a continuum. Our level of maturity is based on where we are located on that spectrum. Sandy Hotchkiss's 2002 book *Why Is It Always About You?: The Seven Deadly Sins of Narcissism* identifies shamelessness, magical thinking, arrogance, envy, entitlement, exploitation, and bad boundaries as the hallmarks of narcissism. Unfortunately, these traits are common in our Western culture. Particularly entitlement, the unreasonable expectation of favourable treatment and automatic compliance without requiring any effort to gain such privilege.

- **Mastery of fears:** Understanding our fears and modulating our reactions to them can play a huge part in achieving personal maturity. We can become easier on ourselves and others, have greater presence in our life, and free up energy for creative and constructive purposes. So why is fear so prevalent and why is it so challenging to manage? We are born to know fear. It is the unavoidable outcome of our awareness of inevitable death. It is at the heart of the cosmic challenge of being spirit in matter and matter inspired—the knowledge that our consciousness and physical self will ultimately and eternally be sundered one from the other. While the knowledge that we have a limited lifespan subtly terrifies us, fear is also essential to preserving life. Primal fear serves to keep us safe, giving the individual incentive to survive and thrive. This is the positive expression of fear; the aspect that reasonably protects us from a reckless expression of the passions and impulses that arise from the equally powerful influence of being a creature driven by the longing for life experience. The interplay of fear and the longing for life creates an effective dynamic balance that sees enough of us reaching maturity while still pushing the edges enough to serve evolution.

There is another type of fear common to humans that does not protect life or support evolution. These are the irrational fears, such as phobias, that can severely impair an individual's capacity to function and are often unconscious. The work of mastery involves bringing the root of the fear to consciousness and taking action to address it.

THE OPPORTUNITY FOR GROWTH

After examining our personal philosophy, we may find aspects that are inconsistent with our spiritual goals or that are not serving us in a way that benefits our lives. The opportunity exists to shift our philosophy to improve the results; however, this is easier said than done. Most humans resist change, preferring the situation we know to one we have never tested.

I know this phenomenon from bitter personal experience, after having spent years at one point in my life in a state of painful dysfunction due to attitudes and beliefs that were skewed in an unhealthy way. It was the pain that finally pushed through my ego resistance and showed me that my worldview was negative, false, and inauthentic. When I accepted this awareness, change came quickly. This is what I call "training by pain," when we accept growth and change only when it is too challenging not to. However, after that first harsh lesson and the subsequent breakthrough, I realized that I needed professional help and education. Freed from my damaging illusions, I moved to a period of growth that I call "training by love." We either stagnate, or change by pain or by love. It is a choice.

A VISION OF OUR FUTURE

Some doubt the value of inquiring into our belief systems, considering it to be self-indulgent contemplation. I believe this inquiry is essential to prepare ourselves for the coming shift. I think of Einstein's famous quote: "We cannot solve our problems with the same thinking we used when we created them." We need a culture that is open, curious, flexible, compassionate, and courageous. This is only possible when enough individuals in our culture exhibit those desired traits. We need a higher level of maturity and responsibility in enough of the population to create change. Preparing for this change, as best we can, is not "navel gazing"—it is "world work" that is critical to our species' survival.

It will be terrifying when crisis comes upon us in the form of infrastructure breakdown, with shortages of essentials (food, water, sanitation, etc.), displacement of peoples from global climate change, and social upheaval. Frightened, confused, and suffering people can turn either to predatory behaviours or to interdependence.

Many factors play into which way a population will evolve when it is in crisis. If a high percentage of the population has reached a compassionate, self-aware state of conscious goodwill, then it is more likely that the crisis can be mitigated, causing less suffering and damage. Those who survive will shape the future of humankind.

If we go forward with the same level of consciousness as our culture presently supports, our only hope is that the trauma of the shift itself will be enough to prompt a great evolution, despite the privations—a training by pain. If the surviving population includes a high percentage of evolved individuals, our species will be in a better position to move forward into a sustainable future that is in alignment with cosmic love.

Glossary

adversarial. The sorting for outcomes based on contesting two or more possible results.

Age of Enlightenment. Also known as the Enlightenment or the Age of Reason, an intellectual and philosophical movement that occurred in Europe, especially Western Europe, in the 17th and 18th centuries CE, with global influences and effects. (See wikipedia.org/wiki/Age_of_Enlightenment.)

alchemy. "An ancient branch of natural philosophy, a philosophical and protoscientific tradition that was historically practised in China, India, the Muslim world, and Europe" (wikipedia.org/wiki/Alchemy). For a more complete description, see Introduction, "Why Alchemy."

anima and animus. In Jungian psychology, a pair of dualistic archetypes that form a union of opposing forces. (See wikipedia.org/wiki/Anima_and_animus.)

archetype. Derived from Jungian psychology, a concept that refers to a universal, inherited idea, pattern of thought, or image that is present in the collective unconscious of all human beings. Archetypes are innate, symbolic, psychological expressions that manifest in response to patterned biological instincts. (See wikipedia.org/wiki/Jungian_archetypes.)

As above, so below. An ancient Sanskrit quote (circa 550 BCE) describing the idea that what happens in a higher realm or plane of existence also happens in a lower realm. It comes from an ancient piece of writing called the Emerald Tablet. The phrase is often associated with Hermeticism. This archaic maxim speaks to the self-similarity, unity, and harmony of the various levels of reality, from the subatomic through to the celestial.

As within, so without. The relationship between our inner and outer worlds. This phrase means that what we see and experience outside of us is influenced by our inner thoughts, feelings, and beliefs. It is considered to be a universal truth or law that shows us the power of our inner world. On the level of identity, this statement suggests that our inner being governs the type of subjective experience we create in our world. This is an important guide to how we might form the kind of world we want to live in.

authenticity / authentic self. Behaving genuinely, dropping the social masks of conditioning, seeking the real self, and living life completely openly and honestly.

Axial Age (circa 800 to 200 BCE). Postulated by Karl Jaspers, an unprecedented upwelling of human intellectual activity that has shaped human thought to this day. (See wikipedia.org/wiki/Axial_Age and wikipedia.org/wiki/Karl_Jaspers.)

BCE. Before Common Era / Before Current Era / Before Christian Era. Used when referring to a year before the birth of Jesus Christ, when the Christian calendar starts counting years.

big man. The term scholars of prehistory use to describe a single, prominent person leading a group. Almost invariably male.

biophilic. Having a bias toward life.

Bronze Age (circa 3300 to 1200 BCE). The period characterized by the use of bronze and other features of early urban civilization.

CE. Common Era / Christian Era. Used when referring to a year after the birth of Jesus Christ, when the Christian calendar starts counting years.

character structure. The manifest physical expression of the body-mind interactions with the environment expressed within the genetic possibilities. The shapings of the body are the results of how the body holds its energetic charge (i.e., holding, blocking, or dissipating the energy).

charge. Available physical energy that is often focused or channelled by emotional excitation.

collective unconscious. "Term introduced by psychiatrist Carl Jung to represent a form of the unconscious (that part of the mind containing memories and impulses of which the individual is not aware) common to mankind as a whole and originating in the inherited structure of the brain. It is distinct from the personal unconscious, which arises from the experience of the individual. According to Jung, the collective unconscious contains archetypes, or universal primordial images and ideas" (britannica.com/science/collective-unconscious). (See also wikipedia.org/wiki/Collective_unconscious.)

conservatism. Commitment to traditional values and ideas, with opposition to change or innovation.

cosmic challenge. To align ourselves with divine cosmic love and, through our actions, contribute to the unfolding and evolution of life.

cosmic consciousness/love. The ground of being; that which gave rise to consciousness and energy, the two primal forces whose separation and reunion were responsible for the Big Bang and the formation of the universe. It comprises both the singularity that predated the Big Bang and the living, dynamic, creative forces of energy and consciousness that have given rise to reality. This force includes all of what is within the cosmos. It appears to be a profound longing to become, a desire for manifestation, and a calling forth of creative potential from whatever mystery preceded space-time into all that it is now and continues to become.

cosmic intelligence. An "ordering force" that set up the "laws of nature," which in turn gave rise to reality; the primordial intelligence that is embedded in all things.

divine, the. Any force or agent involved with the formation and existence of reality; see cosmic consciousness/love.

divine purpose. Intention embedded in a pervasive implicate order; see cosmic consciousness/love.

discernment. The capacity to make successful choices that bring the authentic self into greater resonance with the universe.

enlightenment. A final spiritual state in which everything is understood and there is no more suffering or desire. (To be distinguished from Age of Enlightenment, above.)

epochal shift. A quantum leap of consciousness that changes fundamental human behaviour, self-conception, and how life in our world is perceived.

eukaryote. An organism whose cells have a membrane-bound nucleus, ranging from microscopic single-celled organisms to fungi, seaweeds, plants and animals. (See wikipedia.org/wiki/Eukaryote.)

evil. That which does harm to the unfolding of evolution at any level; a human creation.

fine-tuned universe. "The proposition that the conditions that allow life in the universe can occur only when certain universal dimensionless physical constants lie within a very narrow range of values, so that if any of several fundamental constants were only slightly different, the universe would be unlikely to be conducive to the establishment and development of matter, astronomical structures, elemental diversity, or life as it is understood. Various possible explanations of ostensible fine-tuning are discussed among philosophers, scientists, theologians, and proponents and detractors of creationism. The fine-tuned universe observation is closely related to, but is not exactly synonymous with, the anthropic principle, which is often used as an explanation of apparent fine-tuning" (encyclopedia.pub/entry/27760).

1st millennium BCE. The formative period for the world's religions. (See wikipedia.org/wiki/1st_millennium_BC.)

Ga. Giga-annum, a unit of time equal to one billion years ago.

giant impact theory. An explanation for the origins of our moon, resulting from a roving planet impacting early Earth and blasting a large mass from both bodies, some of which was captured by Earth's gravity. (See wikipedia.org/wiki/Giant-impact_hypothesis.)

Great Purge. Soviet leader Joseph Stalin's large-scale campaign of political repression and murder, from 1936 to 1938. (See wikipedia.org/wiki/Great_Purge.)

grounded. Balanced, realistic, and sensible, with rational or factual support for one's position or attitude.

Hadean period (4.5 Ga). A very early period in Earth's development featuring a solid planetary crust, acidic waters, high temperatures, and a toxic atmosphere—and possibly, at least the building blocks of life. (See wikipedia.org/wiki/Hadean.)

heart / heart wisdom. Seated both literally and figuratively in the centre of the human experience, the heart is the natural balance wheel of all aspects of our experience.

heliocentric. With the Sun at the centre; the structure of our solar system. Controversial when it was identified by Copernicus in the 16th century CE. (See wikipedia.org/wiki/Heliocentrism.)

Hermeticism. The spiritual foundation of alchemy in ancient Alexandria, in the Mediterranean Basin. A syncretism of Egyptian, Greek, and Hebrew wisdom. (See wikipedia.org/wiki/Hermeticism.)

humanism. A Renaissance movement that lifted human beings from being mere servants of God into a more primary position in the scheme of things. (See wikipedia.org/wiki/Renaissance_humanism.)

immortality project. Ernest Becker's term for the human propensity to build a symbolic meaning for ourselves that survives physical death. (See wikipedia.org/wiki/The_Denial_of_Death.)

implicate order. Developed by theoretical physicist David Bohm, a concept that describes a way of simultaneously understanding reality from two different aspects: the perceived (explicate) order of the world and a deeper (implicate) connection between elements. (See wikipedia.org/wiki/Implicate_and_explicate_order.)

Late Heavy Bombardment (4.1 to 3.8 Ga). An event that reshaped Earth's crust, delivering water to a hot planet previously unable to retain moisture. During the Late Heavy Bombardment, it is postulated that Earth was so heavily pummelled by meteorites and comets that almost all of its crust was pulverized into a molten mass. How water was retained on Earth's surface or in its atmosphere remains unknown. (See wikipedia.org/wiki/Late_Heavy_Bombardment.)

love. In the context of this book, refers to the ideal of universal love, agape, unconditional love for all existence that does not depend on filiation or familiarity.

Maslow's hierarchy of needs. A classification system in psychology proposed by Abraham Maslow in 1943, intended to reflect the universal needs of society as its base, then proceeding to more acquired emotions. (See wikipedia.org/wiki/Maslow's_hierarchy_of_needs.)

Migration Period (circa 300 to 600 CE). "Also known as the Barbarian Invasions ... a period in European history marked by large-scale migrations that saw the fall of the Western Roman Empire and subsequent settlement of its former territories by various tribes, and the establishment of the post-Roman kingdoms" (wikipedia.org/wiki/Migration_Period).

mytheme. A template for a human experience or circumstance. In the human collective unconscious (see above), there are generalized templates or scripts for the situations that humans experience, e.g., the morality play, the hero's journey, the revolution, and the struggle to individuate. (See wikipedia.org/wiki/Mytheme.)

nebular hypothesis. The most generally accepted cosmic evolutionary theory, in which the Sun and our solar system were born out of the gravitational collapse of a molecular cloud, forming a large, spinning ball of dust particles and gases that would condense into the planetary bodies. (See wikipedia.org/wiki/Nebular_hypothesis.)

Neolithic period (starting circa 12,000 BCE). The period of prehistory in which humans first took up farming, in the Fertile Crescent, a region of the Middle East. (See wikipedia.org/wiki/Neolithic_Revolution.)

new alchemy. Its intention is to foster a worldview consistent with the observed natural world; it does not contradict scientific knowledge or observed natural phenomena. However, the new alchemy extends beyond what is generally accepted by science and offers a counterperspective to the dismal reductionist philosophy that says there can be no purpose to the universe. The fundamental aim of the new alchemy is to foster a shift in consciousness that will prepare and support humankind to move through the next great evolutionary bottleneck toward a loving, creative, and sustainable state in the future.

overpopulation. Successful reproduction has, since ancient times, been a key element of our species' drive to survive. But the human population now exceeds typical estimates of what can be sustained in the long term, making overpopulation a threat to our survival. (See wikipedia.org/wiki/Sustainable_population.)

Paleolithic period (circa 3.3 million years ago to 11,650 BCE). The prehistoric period in which the use of stone tools came to the fore.

panspermia. The idea that life has been dispersed throughout the universe via asteroids or comets. (See wikipedia.org/wiki/Panspermia).

paradox. A situation or statement that seems impossible or is difficult to understand because it contains two opposite facts or characteristics.

personal mythology. Relates to all the sometimes conflicting thoughts and feelings a person harbours about the world, both consciously and unconsciously, that shape the actions they take and the interpretations they give to their experiences.

Planck epoch. The very earliest moment in the life of the universe, preceding the Big Bang. Currently considered unknowable. (See simple.wikipedia.org/wiki/Planck_epoch.)

presence. The ability to be fully engaged with life in the present moment, while acknowledging the past and the future, but not allowing oneself to be distracted from life by memories of the past or fantasies of the future; being here now and accepting current reality.

prima materia. "In alchemy and philosophy, prima materia ... is the ubiquitous starting material required for the alchemical magnum opus and the creation of the philosopher's stone. It is the primitive formless base of all matter similar to chaos, the quintessence or aether" (wikipedia.org/wiki/Prima_materia).

projection. In psychology, the tendency to ascribe disowned thoughts, feeling, and behaviours onto others while avoiding accepting those traits within ourselves. (See psychologytoday.com/intl/basics/projection.)

Proto-Indo-Europeans. "A hypothetical prehistoric ethnolinguistic group of Eurasia ... [and] reconstructed common ancestor of the Indo-European language family" (wikipedia.org/wiki/Proto-Indo-Europeans).

punctuated equilibrium. A model of evolutionary change that contrasts with gradualism (or slow, consistent, incremental development over time): a more rugged progress through periods of relative stasis, minor change, and then profound radical transformation. (See wikipedia.org/wiki/Punctuated_equilibrium.)

radicalism. The belief that society needs to be changed, and that these changes are only possible through revolutionary means.

Reformation. A 16th-century upheaval in the Christian church. (See wikipedia.org/wiki/Reformation.)

resonance. When the frequency of the initial object's vibration matches the frequency of the second object; to be in alignment with something; a relationship of mutual understanding or trust and agreement.

self-awareness. The capacity to raise the unconscious motivators (memories, core beliefs, fantasies, etc.) of our lives to the conscious level and make choices about them.

self-compassion. The ability to embrace all aspects of life without blaming, punishing, or sabotaging oneself.

self-responsibility. The concept of seeing one's self as the author of one's reality.

shadow. "In analytical psychology, the shadow ... is an unconscious aspect of the personality that does not correspond with the ego ideal, which tends to cause the ego to resist and project the shadow, creating conflict with it" (wikipedia.org/wiki/Shadow_(psychology)). In short, the shadow is the self's emotional blind spot, the part the ego does not want to acknowledge. It is not necessarily bad or negative, just unacknowledged as an aspect of self.

social isolation. An unnatural condition for human beings; being part of a community is our natural state. (See wikipedia.org/wiki/Social_isolation.)

soul. Typically used to describe the personalized spark of the divine within an individual.

spirit. The discrete unit or node of psycho-energetic essence within the individual; the point of fundamental connection to the greater non-tangible world. Similar to soul.

spiritual alchemy. A transmutation of life experience to create the "gold" of conscious evolution.

spirituality. The nature of the individual's relationship to the intangibles of life and the cosmos; any belief system that represents the individual's point of view on these matters falls under the category of spirituality, whether it be religion, agnosticism, or atheism. Ultimately the expression of our spirituality is in how we live our lives and how successfully we align ourselves with divine purpose.

teleology. A belief that there is a purpose to the cosmos and all that is in it.

transmutation. A key alchemical principle that states reality can be altered by a sufficiently advanced practitioner. While this concept fails on the physical plane (transmutation of metals), it remains valid for the transformations of emotions, attitudes, ideas, and societies.

unconscious. "The complex of mental activities within an individual that proceed without [their] awareness" (britannica.com/science/unconscious).

worldview. "The fundamental cognitive orientation of a society, a subgroup, or even an individual. It encompasses natural philosophy, fundamental existential and normative postulates or themes, values (often conflicting), emotions, and ethics ..." (Gary B. Palmer, *Toward a Theory of Cultural Linguistics* (University of Texas Press, 1996), p. 114.)

About the Author

Brad Cassidy was born March 1955 on Thetis Island in British Columbia, Canada. He spent his youth exploring the rugged coastal terrain and worked as a forestry consultant for many years in what is now called Haida Gwaii, an archipelago off British Columbia's west coast. He travelled extensively during that time in Asia, India, the South Pacific Islands, Australia, New Zealand, and the Middle East. In 1995 he moved to the Vancouver Lower Mainland to focus on the study and practice of personal development. He worked as a personal development consultant and called his practice Heart Wisdom. Brad spent the last ten years of his life researching and writing this book. He had a passion for supporting the evolution of human consciousness.

www.ingramcontent.com/pod-product-compliance
Lightning Source LLC
Chambersburg PA
CBHW020405080526
44584CB00014B/1180